FABULOUS FLOWERS

Mini-Quilts in Dimensional Appliqué

SHARON K BAKER

Martingale® & COMPANY

Fabulous Flowers: Mini-Quilts in Dimensional Appliqué
© 2005 by Sharon K Baker

That Patchwork Place® is an imprint of
Martingale & Company®.

Martingale & Company
20205 144th Avenue NE
Woodinville, WA 98072-8478 USA
www.martingale-pub.com

Credits

President · *Nancy J. Martin*
CEO · *Daniel J. Martin*
VP and General Manager · *Tom Wierzbicki*
Publisher · *Jane Hamada*
Editorial Director · *Mary V. Green*
Managing Editor · *Tina Cook*
Technical Editor · *Darra Williamson*
Copy Editor · *Melissa Bryan*
Design Director · *Stan Green*
Illustrator · *Robin Strobel*
Cover Designer · *Shelly Garrison*
Text Designer · *Trina Craig*
Photographer · *Brent Kane*

Mission Statement

Dedicated to providing quality products and service
to inspire creativity.

Printed in China
10 09 08 07 06 05   8 7 6 5 4 3 2 1

Library of Congress Cataloging-in-Publication Data

Baker, Sharon K
    Fabulous flowers : mini-quilts in dimensional appliqué /
Sharon K Baker.
        p. cm.
    ISBN 1-56477-610-7
    1. Appliqué—Patterns. 2. Quilting. 3. Album quilts.
4. Miniature quilts. 5. Flowers in art. I. Title.
    TT779.B 35 2005
    746.46'041—dc22
                                        2005012745

Dedication

To my Grandma Johnson and my mother, Mary. They have been my greatest supporters. Without their loving words of encouragement, I would not be the artist I am today.

I would also like to thank my sister, Kathy, for signing me up for my first quilting class. Because of that class I discovered my passion for quilting and fiber arts.

I will forever be grateful for the people in my life who believed in me and supported my occasionally compulsive behavior.

I would like to thank my husband, Chuck, for helping me realize my dreams.

And a final thank-you to Martingale & Company for giving me this wonderful opportunity.

CONTENTS

INTRODUCTION

I'VE ADMIRED BALTIMORE album quilts for a long time. The beautiful colors and fine needlework make these quilts true works of art. Victorian women worked very hard to perfect the needle arts with studies of botanicals. Well-educated women studied carefully, in detail, the flowers and birds around them, and recorded their observations in album quilts. Each symbol in a quilt represented something special to the quiltmaker. I started this book wanting to make Baltimore album quilts with a modern twist. The sewing machine has opened up a world of possibilities.

Our world moves at such a hurried pace that we rarely have time to stop and smell the flowers, much less create them. I hope you'll have fun using my methods to create flowers that look so real you can almost smell them. Using nature as your inspiration, you will create wonderfully realistic flowers to use in any quilt or wearable art project. This book was designed to open up unlimited

possibilities for using fabric, beads, and embellishing threads in creative and imaginative ways.

I've been a crafting gypsy all my life, going from one craft to another until I found quilting. Quilting is my true calling. I brought many of my past crafting skills into my quilting, so many of the things I do may seem unconventional. Quilting with no rules is so freeing! One of the things I do that I'm sure will shock and surprise most quilters is that I quilt the background fabric before I appliqué the other elements of the quilt.

All the flowers in this book are constructed using the same basic instructions. The process may seem intimidating at first, but after you construct your first flower, you'll see that these flowers are very easy to make. Trying something new can be frustrating at first, but when you accomplish what you set out to do, the rewards are well worth the effort. I've worked on making the flowers and leaves in this book quick and easy. The directions are only guidelines; explore your own creativity and style. Enjoy the process.

When you sew a strip of petals, I suggest that you make more than the directions call for. That way, you'll always have a great stash for making flowers or leaves in future projects. I like to spend an hour or so making petals of all colors without really knowing where I'll end up using them. I figure if I'm going to sit at the sewing machine, I might as well make as many petals as I can. I also do this when I quilt a project; I have several quilt squares layered and ready to go. I think it's so much easier to set up the machine for quilting and get as many squares done as I can. This is also true when I make fabric strips for stems; I make yard after yard. That way, when I need a few stems, I just go to my stash and get what I need for that project. Having a ready selection of flower petals, leaves, and stems makes the whole process more enjoyable. I can easily go to my stash and whip up a quick gift for a special someone.

TOOLS AND SUPPLIES

You won't need all the supplies mentioned in this list for every project, but it's a good idea to read through the list to make sure you have the items on hand. Each project includes a detailed list of the specific supplies you'll need for that quilt.

Fabric: Use only quality cotton fabric for making the flowers in this book. I use hand-dyed or batik fabrics because of the wonderful shading in the colors. You'll only need small amounts of fabric, so spending a little extra on hand-dyed or batik fabrics won't break the bank, and the overall look of the quilt will reflect the quality of the fabric. Avoid buying inexpensive fabrics, because they tend to fray easily, making them very difficult to work with. I work on my designs with the idea that someday someone may think of my quilts as heirlooms; if I use fabrics of lesser quality, the fabric may not stand the test of time.

Batting: Use good-quality cotton or polyester batting. Some quilters prefer cotton batting exclusively, but I've found that the polyester batting on the market today is wonderful. I'm not talking about the fluffy polyester battings from the 1970s, but the woven polyester that looks and feels like cotton batting—that is, thin and dense. You'll use small scraps of batting for the quilts in this book, so use what you have on hand. If you don't already have a supply of batting, buy a crib-size batting and cut it into small pieces as needed.

Beads: Beads can be found in craft stores, bead shops, and online. I prefer glass beads, and I enjoy finding the perfect bead to match the flower. I avoid plastic and metal beads because the beads may discolor the fabric over time. Purchase the best-quality beads you can find. Packages of less-expensive beads often contain defective and broken beads.

Beware: buying beads can become addictive! I store my beads in the small, resealable plastic bags sold in bead stores, and then put the bags into floss boxes by color. This keeps the beads organized and easy to find. Bead shops also sell bead organizers for small collections. However you store your beads, avoid extreme temperature changes and humidity. If stored correctly, the beads will last forever.

Hand-sewing needles: I use size 12 quilting "Between" needles for everything. These needles are short and strong, making them easy to push through thick layers of fabric. The eye of the needle is small enough that most beads will slide on with ease.

I recommend using any needle you're comfortable with. (Some quilters like to appliqué with a longer needle.) Buy the best-quality needles you can find, and treat yourself to a new one after you've used a needle for eight hours. Nothing is sweeter and will make your sewing experience more pleasurable than a needle with a sharp point and smooth shaft gliding easily through the fabric.

Machine-sewing needles: For the best results, use needles that are recommended by your machine manufacturer. I use microtex needles for piecing and quilting because they are sharp and fine. Batik fabrics are very densely woven, and these needles handle them well. When I'm quilting the background fabric on a quilt, I use a machine-quilting needle.

Machine-piecing thread: Cotton thread works best, although you can also use cotton-wrapped polyester. I use 50-weight threads for all piecing.

Quality thread is critical to a long-lasting quilt. Never use old thread. If you're unsure how old a spool of thread might be, don't use it. Many of us have thread that has been passed down from our grandmothers, but despite its sentimental value, I recommend you not use this thread on any quilting project. Thread has a life span, and it would be awful to have a project fall apart because of old thread.

Quilting and topstitching threads: Manufacturers assign numbers to thread weights. The larger the number, the finer the thread. Topstitching thread is usually 35- or 40-weight. Quilting thread is usually 40-weight, but almost any type of thread can be used for quilting, including 50-weight. Embroidery thread is usually 60-weight, and so on.

Heavier quilting thread sits on the surface of the quilt top more than finer thread. Sometimes you want the quilting to show, and sometimes you want the quilting to just blend into the background fabric. Play around with different thread weights until you find the look you like.

Embellishing threads: It is mind-boggling how many embellishing threads there are on the market today. Almost any type of embroidery, cross-stitch, knitting, or crochet thread will work for the projects in this book. Embellishing thread can be purchased from craft and needle-art stores. Small amounts of embellishing threads are available on color-coded cards.

Bias-tape makers: I like to make vines and stems from bias strips since I can curve them any way I wish. I use a bias-tape maker to make these bias vines and stems. There are several brands and types of tape makers on the market, and in my experience they all work well. I use the ¼" and ⅜" sizes to make perfect stems and vines.

Acid-free, water-soluble glue: Gluing the stems in place in preparation for appliqué is a great time-saver. I use a needle-tip applicator to apply small dots of acid-free, water-soluble glue to the back of the bias tape to baste the stems in place. I take care not to apply the glue too thickly or it becomes very difficult to push the needle through the edge of the stem. I prefer to hand appliqué the stems, but you can use any method you like.

Rulers: A 6" x 24" ruler and a 15" square ruler are handy. Any brand will work for these projects.

Rotary cutter and mat: Again, any brand will work. Just make sure the blade in your cutter is sharp.

Scissors: You will need a good, sharp pair of fabric scissors to cut out the flower petals. I use a medium-sized pair.

Tube/point turner: You will need a small tube/point turner for turning the flower petals and leaves right side out. You can find one of these in the notions section of your local fabric store. I use one that is a clear plastic tube with a metal rod.

Resealable plastic bags: I store almost everything in resealable plastic bags; they keep me organized. The bags come in several sizes and are very inexpensive. You can find small ones at most craft stores, and the grocery store has small, snack-sized bags that are extremely versatile. These bags are a great way to store small bits of embellishing thread, beads, and cut fabric. I also store all my flower petals and leaves in them.

BASIC QUILT CONSTRUCTION

Unlike standard appliqué quilts, these projects require that you quilt—and often bind—the quilt top before adding the appliquéd flowers. The following pages provide the information you'll need to construct the backdrop for your floral appliqués.

Selecting the Background Fabric

The fabric you select for the background of your quilt is an important choice. When you look at the quilt, the background should be just that—in the background. The color should complement your overall design, not overwhelm it.

I like the background to suggest that something is going on just out of view or that the sun is shining behind the design. A solid or solid-looking fabric is the most effective.

It's best to audition the background fabric by laying the other elements on top of it and then viewing everything from five or six feet away. If the fabrics have good contrast and I like the way they look together, I go for it.

When you've chosen the fabric that you like for the background, cut two pieces: one for the front of the quilt and one for the back. (Yes, the back of the quilt matters!) Cut the fabric and batting 1" or so larger than the desired finished size

of the quilt on all sides because the layers will draw up as you quilt. The extra batting and fabric allow you to square up the quilt after the quilting is done. See page 8 for more information on batting.

Basting the Layers

This is one of the most important steps for ensuring a smooth, flat quilt. Lay out the backing fabric wrong side up on a clean, flat surface and smooth out any wrinkles in the fabric. Center the batting on top of the backing and ease out any lumps or bumps. Place the quilt top right side up on the batting and smooth all the layers, making sure everything is flat and even.

There are several ways to baste the layers of your quilt together. You can use thread and a large running stitch in a grid pattern, or you can use size #1 brass safety pins, which is my preference. You can find these pins at any quilt store. Start in the center of the quilt and work outward. Place the pins about a fist's width apart, smoothing the quilt layers as you go. Be sure to pin the corners and edges of the quilt. Turn the quilt over and make sure the backing is still smooth and flat.

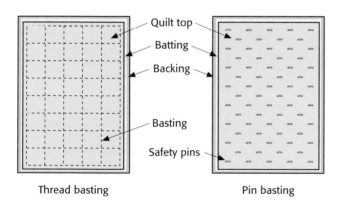

Thread basting   Pin basting

Choosing a Quilting Design

Now that the layers of your quilt are basted together, you must think about the quilting design. Quilting adds texture, and simple designs work best for the projects in this book. I like to stipple and echo quilt, and I also use swirls, loops, and other uncomplicated designs. You can make quilting look like sun rays, rain, wind, leaves, grass, or branches in the distance.

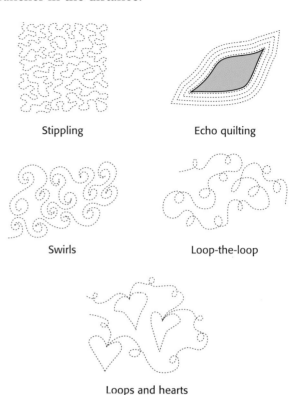

Stippling   Echo quilting

Swirls   Loop-the-loop

Loops and hearts

If you keep the quilting design simple, you won't need to mark the quilt top for quilting. You're limited only by your imagination, so let yourself go and enjoy the process. Doodle on paper until you find a design that you think will work for your quilt. There are also dozens of books on machine quilting that contain many ideas for quilting designs.

Save your doodles for future reference. They can be a great source of inspiration for later projects.

Quilting the Layers

I like to machine quilt my quilts because it's fast and easy. Since it's almost impossible to quilt around the flowers once they have been appliquéd to the background, I prefer to quilt the background fabric before the flowers and stems are appliquéd in place. If you prefer, you can appliqué the stems to the background and then echo quilt around them, or you can hand quilt the project, either before or after the flowers and stems have been appliquéd in place.

Squaring Up the Quilt

After you've quilted the quilt, you must square it up. Starting in one corner of the quilt, straighten the two sides by trimming them with a square ruler and rotary cutter. Move to the opposite corner and square up the remaining two sides. Check the corners against each other to make sure that the sides are straight and true. Adjust them as needed.

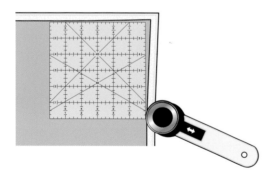

Binding the Quilt

The binding on a quilt is like a frame. Choice of binding fabric is important; it should somehow relate to the body of the quilt in color or design. I like to use one of the fabrics in the quilt for the binding. Since all the quilts in this book are small, and either square or rectangular, I can usually use one double-fold, straight-of-grain fabric strip for the binding. I cut the strip 2½" wide across the fabric width (from selvage to selvage). With wrong sides together, I fold the strip in half to measure 1¼" wide and press down the length of the strip. If I need more than one strip of binding for my quilt, I join the binding strips end to end and press the seams open.

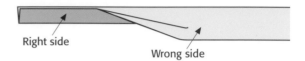

Right side

Wrong side

1. Align the raw edge of the binding with the raw edge of your quilt. Leave 5" or 6" of the binding free and start sewing in the middle of one side of the quilt with a ⅜"-wide seam allowance. Stop sewing ⅜" from the corner.

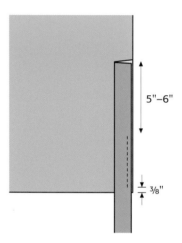

5"–6"

⅜"

2. Turn the quilt counterclockwise 90°. Fold the binding up to form a 45° angle. Fold the binding back down on itself, aligning the raw edges of the binding and the quilt.

3. Start stitching on the edge of the quilt. Repeat with the remaining corners.

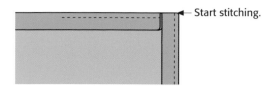

Start stitching.

4. Stop stitching about 5" from where you want to join the ends of the binding. Remove the quilt from the machine. Fold one end of the binding back on itself about 2". Fold the other end of the binding back on itself. Butt the folded ends together and crease the fold.

Butt the folds together.

5. Unfold the binding. With right sides together, line up the crease and sew directly on the crease line. Test the strip to make sure it fits without any excess fabric. Trim the excess binding ¼" from the seam and press the seam open.

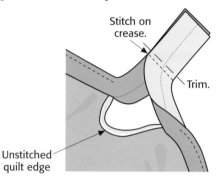

Stitch on crease.

Trim.

Unstitched quilt edge

6. Finish sewing the binding to the quilt. Fold the binding over the raw edge of the quilt and stitch it to the back of the quilt with a blind stitch. The folded binding will form a miter at each corner. Secure the corners on the front of the quilt with a few blind stitches.

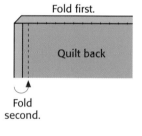

Fold first.

Quilt back

Fold second.

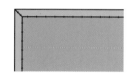

FLOWER CONSTRUCTION

WHEN WORKING WITH flowers, it's a good idea to have a basic understanding of flower anatomy. Without getting too technical, here are a few terms I use in the book that may or may not be familiar to you.

Flower Anatomy

Petal: The leaflike part of a flower

Stamen: The pollen-bearing part of a flower

Calyx: The flower parts that make up the outer circle; they are usually green, but they can be brightly colored. When the outer petals are joined they are called a calyx.

Stem: The part of the plant that supports leaves and flowers

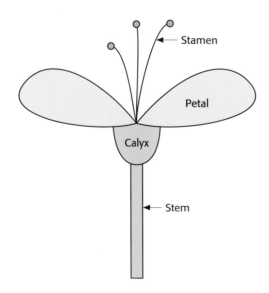

Leaves are usually green and grow from the stem of a plant. Although leaf shapes can be very complex, all leaves have the same basic construction.

Stem: The part of a leaf that connects it to the plant

Center vein: The main artery of the leaf, which runs from the stem to the leaf tip

Side veins: The smaller veins that branch off the main artery

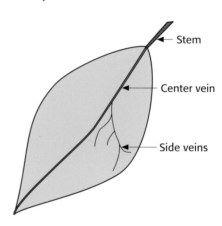

Making Basic Flower Petals

MOST OF the flowers in this book are constructed from strips of fabric. The basic flower petal and the same basic construction process are used to make many of these flowers. The example given here uses 3" x 22" strips to construct the basic flower petal. This is a common size; however, some projects call for slightly wider or narrower strips, and the petals will vary in size accordingly.

1. Cut two 3" x 22" strips of fabric and layer them with right sides together. Fold the strips in half to measure 1½" x 22", and iron a crease down the length to mark the center. Unfold the strips, but keep them layered.

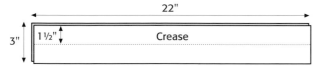

Place strips right sides together.

2. Put thread to match your fabric in the top and bobbin of your sewing machine. (It amazes me how many sewers use a different-colored thread in the bobbin. For this technique, it's very important to have matching thread; the seams on the petals may show and you wouldn't want an odd-colored thread to be visible.) Set your machine to a very short stitch length—about 1.5 or less on some machines, or 15 to 20 stitches per inch on others.

3. Starting at one end of the layered strip set, insert the needle into the fabric and begin to sew one side of a petal shape. Stop with the needle in the down position when you reach the center crease. Lift the presser foot, pivot the fabric, and sew the other side of the petal to the desired width, stopping at the raw edge of the fabric strip.

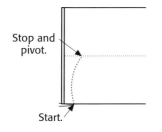
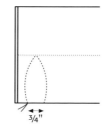

4. Lift the presser foot. Pivot the fabric and, beginning about ½" from the first petal, start sewing up to the center of the strip again. Don't cut the threads between petals and don't worry about slight variations in your petal shapes. Variety in the shapes is what makes the flowers look natural. It's more important to keep the spacing consistent between the petals to make sure you have an adequate seam allowance.

5. Continue making petals ½" apart across the length of the strip until you reach the end, and then turn the fabric to begin sewing petals along the other side of the strip. Alternate the petal shapes so they interlock like teeth between the petals on the other side of the strip, leaving ½" between the tops of the petals. Continue stitching petals across the length of the strip.

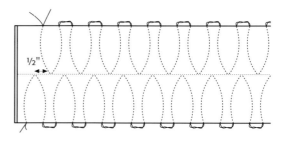

6. Using a sharp pair of fabric scissors, cut out the petals adding a scant ¼"-wide seam allowance. Just don't cut *too* close to the stitching or when you turn the petals right side out, you'll push through the seam.

7. Use a point turner to turn the petals right side out, and finger-press them into shape. Store the petals in a resealable plastic bag until you're ready to assemble them into flowers.

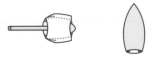

8. Thread a hand-sewing needle with a double strand of matching-colored thread. Stitch about ¼" from the raw edges of the petals to string them together. When you have the appropriate number of petals on your thread, loop around and join the petals, pulling the thread snug while pushing the raw edges of the petals to the back of the flower. Stitch through the raw edges on the back of the flower petals several times to lock the shape, and then knot the thread.

Making Hump-Shaped Petals

THE PROCESS for sewing hump-shaped petals is very similar to the technique used for sewing the basic flower petal, as described in the preceding section. You can use hump-shaped petals to make several different types of flowers. The example given here uses 4" x 22" strips to construct the hump-shaped flower petal. This is a common size; however, some projects call for slightly wider or narrower strips, and the petals will vary in size accordingly. Follow the same basic instructions to make any hump-shaped flower petals, and then assemble them following the instructions given for the specific flowers you're making.

1. Cut two 4" x 22" strips of fabric and layer them with right sides together. Fold the strips in half to measure 2" x 22", and iron a crease down the length to mark the center. Unfold the strips, but keep them layered.

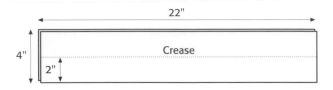

2. Put thread to match your fabric in the top and bobbin of your sewing machine. Set your machine to a very short stitch length—about 1.5 or less on some machines, or 15 to 20 stitches per inch on others.

3. Starting at one end of the layered strip set, insert the needle into the fabric, and begin to sew a humped-petal shape. When you're ¼" from the crease, turn and begin the opposite side of the petal, pivoting the fabric to maintain a smooth, curved seam. It takes a little practice to sew a smooth curve, but it isn't hard to master. I've found that if I sew a little faster then normal it's much easier to keep the top of the hump smooth.

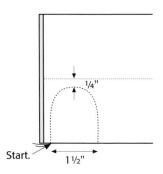

4. Sew the petal to the desired width; lift the presser foot. Pivot the fabric and, beginning about ½" from the first petal, start sewing up to the center of the strip again. Don't cut the threads between petals and don't worry about slight variations in your petal shapes. Variety in the shapes is what makes the flowers look

natural. It's more important to keep the spacing consistent between the petals.

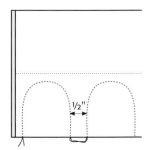

5. Continue making petals ½" apart across the length of the strip until you reach the end; turn the fabric to begin sewing petals along the other side of the strip. Be sure to leave ½" between the tops of the petals. Continue stitching petals across the length of the strip.

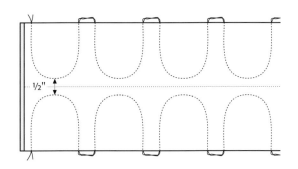

6. Using a sharp pair of fabric scissors, cut out the petals adding a scant ¼"-wide seam allowance. Don't cut too close to the stitching or when you turn the petals right side out, you'll push through the seam.

7. Use a point turner to turn the petals right side out, and finger-press them into shape. Store the petals in a resealable plastic bag until you're ready to assemble them into flowers.

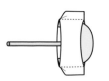

8. Thread a hand-sewing needle with a double strand of matching-colored thread. Stitch about ¼" from the raw edges of the petals to string them together. When you have the appropriate number of petals on your thread, loop around and join the petals, pulling the thread snug while pushing the raw edges of the petals to the back of the flower. Stitch through the raw edges on the back of the flower petals several times to lock the shape, and then knot the thread.

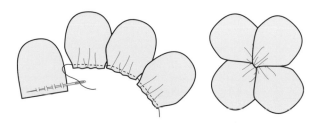

Making a Calyx from a Hump-Shaped Petal

You can use a single hump-shaped petal to make a quick and easy calyx on almost any flower in this book. By making simple adjustments in the size of the hump shape, you can make any flower into a bud.

1. To prepare the calyx, follow the directions for making the basic hump-shaped petal (page 16). Cut out the petal, turn it right side out, and finger-press it into shape. Finger-press a slight (⅛"-wide) hem along the bottom edge of the petal.

⅛" hem

2. Insert the raw edges of a flower or flower bud into the prepared calyx. Make sure all the raw edges of the flower are covered by the calyx.

3. Thread a hand-sewing needle with thread to match the calyx. Blind stitch the calyx to the flower along the folded edge, pulling the thread to slightly gather.

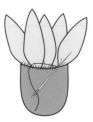

Making Stems

I MAKE bias tape for the flower stems on my quilts. A ¼"- or ⅜"-wide bias-tape maker (see page 9 of "Tools and Supplies") makes the process quick and easy. For most of the projects in this book the materials list calls for ¼-yard cuts of fabric for the stems. This yardage allows you to cut 12"-long bias strips. Cut as many strips as you need to total the required length for the project you're making.

MAKING BIAS TAPE

1. Position a ruler with the 45° angle marking lined up along the selvage end of the fabric. (The side of the ruler will be on the bias of the fabric.) Use a rotary cutter to cut the fabric to the desired width. Cut strips ½" wide to make ¼"-wide bias tape. To make ⅜"-wide bias tape, cut strips ¾" wide. Cut as many strips as needed.

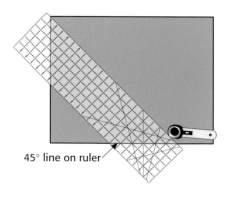

45° line on ruler

2. Spray the strips of fabric with starch. (Allow the fabric to absorb the starch or the starch will flake.) Insert the strip of fabric into the tape maker. As you pull the fabric through the tape maker, press with a steam iron. I press the fabric strips on a hard surface; this keeps the creased edges of the tape sharp and crisp. Allow the fabric to cool before you remove it from the pressing surface.

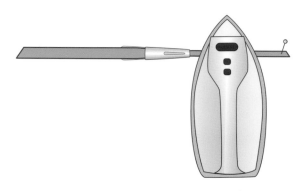

3. Cut the tape into stems as needed. If you need ⅛"-wide tape, just fold the ¼"-wide tape in half and press.

⅛"

MAKING A CALYX WITH A BIAS STRIP
Leftover bias strips can be used to make a calyx.

1. Cut a leftover ¾"-wide bias strip into 1½"-long sections. Fold under a slight hem on each 1½" edge; press.

2. Wrap the front side of the flower with the prepared fabric strip. Make sure the calyx fabric covers the raw edges of the flower or bud shapes.

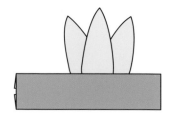

3. Thread a hand-sewing needle with thread to match the calyx. Blind stitch the calyx to the front of the flower.

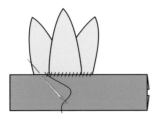

4. Bring one end of the calyx to the back of the flower, making sure the hem of the calyx covers the raw edge of the flower; stitch the calyx in place.

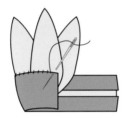

5. Bring the other end of the calyx to the back of the flower, and trim the strip if necessary, leaving enough to make a scant hem. Finish stitching the calyx to the flower and blind stitch the hemmed end to secure.

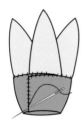

6. Go back through the calyx and flower several times to make sure all the edges are secure, pulling the thread slightly to gather. Knot the thread on the back of the flower.

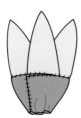

Making Leaves

LEAVES ARE an important part of a good overall design. Never underestimate the power of a simple leaf. Here are several options for making leaves.

MAKING BASIC LEAVES

When making these leaves, keep the form simple. Complex shapes are difficult to turn right side out smoothly. The example given here uses 4" x 22" strips to construct the basic leaf. Some projects call for slightly wider or narrower strips, and the leaves will vary in size accordingly.

1. Cut two 4" x 22" strips of fabric and layer them with right sides together. Fold the strips in half to measure 2" x 22", and iron a crease down the length to mark the center. Unfold the strips, but keep them layered.

2. Put thread to match your fabric in the top and bobbin of your sewing machine. Set your machine to a very short stitch length—about 1.5 or less on some machines, or 15 to 20 stitches per inch on others.

3. Starting at one end of the layered strip set, insert the needle into the fabric, and begin to sew one side of a simple leaf shape. Stop with the needle in the down position when you reach the center crease. Lift the presser foot, pivot the fabric, and sew the other side of the leaf, stopping at the raw edge of the fabric strip.

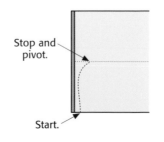

4. Lift the presser foot. Pivot the fabric and, beginning about ½" from the first leaf, start sewing up to the center of the strip again. Don't cut the threads between leaves and don't worry about slight variations in your leaf shapes. Variety in the shapes is what makes the leaves look natural. It's more im-portant to keep the spacing consistent between the leaves.

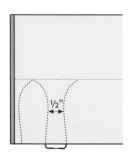

5. Continue making leaves ½" apart across the length of the strip until you reach the end, and then turn the fabric to begin sewing leaves along the other side of the strip. Alternate the leaf shapes so they interlock like teeth between the leaves on the other side of the strip, leaving ½" between the tops of the leaves. Continue stitching leaves across the length of the strip.

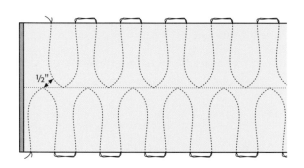

6. Using a sharp pair of fabric scissors, cut out the leaves adding a scant ¼"-wide seam allowance. Don't cut too close to the stitching or when you turn the leaves right side out, you'll push through the seam.

7. Use a point turner to turn the leaves right side out, and finger-press them into shape. Store the leaves in a resealable plastic bag until you're ready to use them.

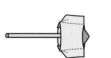

8. Thread a hand-sewing needle with a double strand of matching-colored thread. Finger-press a slight hem along the bottom edge of the leaf. Stitch the opening closed with a run-ning stitch, and pull the thread to gather the bottom edge of the leaf. If the leaf will be covered by a stem or flower, you can leave the bottom edge raw.

MAKING FUSED LEAVES

Fused leaves are two-sided and flexible. Although their shapes can be complex, these leaves are very easy to make.

1. Cut two pieces of fabric about 1" larger than the desired leaf design. Following the manu-facturer's instructions, fuse the fabric wrong sides together using heavyweight, sewable fusible web. Allow the fabric to cool.

2. Trace the leaf shape onto the fabric using your favorite marking tool or method.

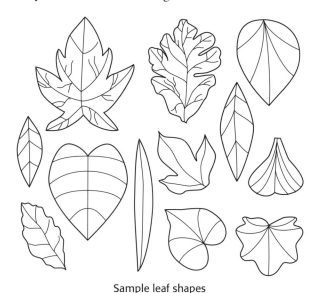

Sample leaf shapes

3. Set your sewing machine to a short stitch length—about 1.5 or less on some machines, or 15 to 20 stitches per inch on others. Put thread that matches or contrasts with the leaf fabric in the top and bobbin. Stitch the center vein and all the side veins of the leaf. Go around the edge of the leaf to jump to the side veins.

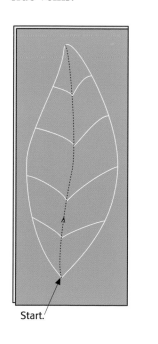
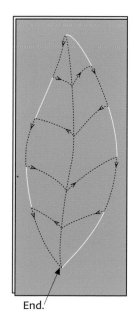

Start. End.

4. Reset your machine to a small zigzag stitch. Starting at the bottom of the leaf (where the stem will be), stitch around the leaf's outside edge, pivoting at any points. Stop, pivot, and stitch up the stem, and then turn the leaf to stitch over the stem a second time for added thickness. Backstitch several times to lock your stitching.

5. Use a sharp pair of fabric scissors to cut out the leaf close to—but not through—the outside stitching. Press the leaf with steam to set the stitches.

6. Stitch the leaf in place. Since it is finished on both sides, you only need to tack it down in a few places. If you like, put a few tucks in the leaf for a more realistic look.

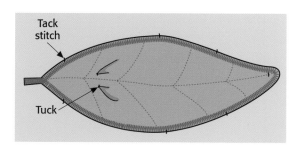

Tack stitch

Tuck

Making Yo-Yos

THE SIMPLE and versatile yo-yo has been around since the nineteenth century. I love making yo-yos! I've come up with several types of flowers that you can make using these simple circles of fabric. Let's explore some methods for making yo-yos.

CUTTING FABRIC CIRCLES

To quickly and easily cut circles from fabric, cut a strip of fabric as wide as the desired diameter of the finished circle, 2" for example. Subcut the strip into squares and use a sharp pair of fabric scissors to trim the squares into circles. Don't worry about making perfect circles; once the fabric is gathered, the circles will look perfect.

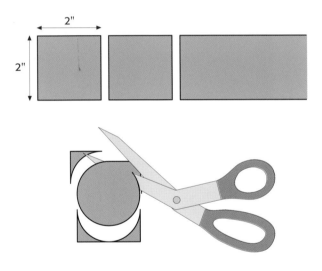

MAKING BASIC YO-YOS

Use a running stitch to hand stitch a scant ¼" hem around your prepared circle. Stitch closer to the raw edge of the circle than to the folded edge. Pull the thread tightly to gather the center of the circle with the right side of the fabric facing out. Use your fingers to flatten and distribute the gathers around the circle. Stitch through a few gathers to lock the shape. Push the thread to the wrong side

of the circle and make a knot. Sew the yo-yo to the quilt with the gathered side up.

MAKING RAW-EDGED YO-YOS

On the right side of the yo-yo fabric, hand sew a running stitch around the outside edge of the circle, about ¼" from the raw edge. Pull the thread tightly to gather the center of the circle. Use your fingers to flatten and distribute the gathers. Tie off the thread, hiding the knot inside the circle. Sew the yo-yo to the quilt with the gathered side down.

Beading

Some of the quilts include beading as an embellishment, usually in the flower centers. In some cases the beads are glued in place. In other instances, the beads are added individually using a stab stitch, or are strung and couched to the quilt by hand as described in "Couching Threads for Embellishment" (page 23). The individual project instructions will tell you the number, color, and type of beads to use, and suggest which method to use for attaching them.

Couching Threads for Embellishment

COUCHING IS a method of attaching almost any thread, including heavy or highly textured threads or yarns, to the surface of fabric by using a finer thread to work small stitches over the embellishing thread. You can couch by hand or machine and you can use a contrasting or matching thread over the top, depending on the look you want.

To hand stitch, use a simple running stitch over the top of the embellishing thread.

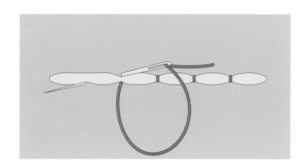

Use a straight stitch or a zigzag stitch to machine stitch the embellishing thread in place.

DECORATIVE PIN

After making a project, you may have some leftover flowers and leaves. Why not make them into a decorative pin? This is a very quick and fun project to make. It really only takes minutes and makes a wonderful gift.

Making the Pin

CHOOSE AND make your favorite flower and a few leaves to go with it. Stitch the leaves to the back of the flower, making sure to hide the raw edges behind the flower petals. If you like, you can stitch several flowers together to make a really nice arrangement. Play with several different combinations of flowers and leaves—the possibilities are endless. Use a double strand of matching thread to hand stitch a pin attachment to the back of the arrangement. You can find these notions in any craft or bead store.

GARDEN TOUR

ADDING A FEW flowers to a project can make a simple quilt simply stunning. The quilts shown in this gallery are made using the flowers from this book.

"GRANDMA'S FLOWER GARDEN"
17½" x 9½"
I made this quilt to honor my grandmother. She was a wonderful gardener and a great influence in my life.
The picket fence represents the American ideal of happiness.

"CABIN IN THE WOODS"
11" x 11"
I made this quilt using a preprinted panel, and I beaded the cabin after the quilting was finished. I think the results are stunning. The beads add a touch of light and interest.

"CABIN IN THE WOODS 2"
11½" x 11½"
After making my first "Cabin in the Woods" (above), I became obsessed with finding more preprinted cabin panels. I beaded the cabin after it was quilted, and pulled the colors of the flowers from the greenery in the panel.

"THE SHY GEISHA"
12½" x 19"

I found this preprinted panel and knew instantly what to do with it. I made this quilt for my mother, who loves all things Asian. My younger sister was born in Japan and I thought this would be a great reminder of that time in our lives. I beaded the quilt after it was quilted, creating flowers that echo the colors in the panel.

"GEISHA"
11½" x 11½"

This panel was part of the geisha print I used for "The Shy Geisha" (above). I decided to make this one rather dark and mysterious. It's amazing how just changing the colors created such a huge difference in the appearance of the two quilts.

"FLOWERS IN THE GRASS"
8½" x 5"

I became obsessed with embellishing threads and wanted a way to use as many different varieties as I could in a project. I couched the embellishing threads and quilted the piece at the same time. This project was a lot of fun.

"FLOWERS IN THE GRASS 2"
6" x 9"

After making the first "Flowers in the Grass" (above), I felt I needed to explore the idea further. This project has a totally different feel to it. I love the whimsy the embellishing threads provide.

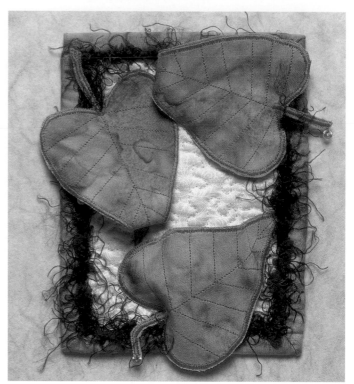

"Leaf Study 1"
4½" x 6"
When I was working on the idea for "Falling Leaves"
(page 93), I wanted to explore some other leaf options.
This project was the beginning of a weeklong
obsession with leaves. I added clear beads to the leaves
to represent the rain.

"Topiary"
6" x 11"
The topiary is a Victorian garden ornament.
I wanted to make a small but sweet version of the
topiary using ribbon, beads, embellishing threads,
fused leaves, and a few fanciful flowers.

"Leaf Study 2"
6" x 5"
The dark blue background—which I thought
looked stormy—gives this quilt a totally different feel
from "Leaf Study 1" (above right). I didn't use
any beads on this project.

"LEAF STUDY 3"
5" x 9"
The leaves in this project are quite intricate.
I used a batik fabric with lots of fall colors and added
a few beads for raindrops.

"LEAF STUDY 4"
6½" x 9"
I found this mottled brown batik fabric that I thought
looked just like the color of fall leaves. I really like the
contrast of the dark leaves on the light background.

STAR FLOWERS

This flower truly is a star! It's the easiest of all the flowers to make.
If you change the color of the petals or the flower center, you can create a new flower.
The variations are endless.

FINISHED SIZE: 6" x 6"

Materials

Materials are based on fabric that measures 42" wide.

- 2 squares, 8" x 8", of mottled blue fabric for background and backing
- 1 strip, 2½" x 42", of golden yellow fabric for binding and yo-yo flower centers
- 2 strips, 2" x 22", of yellow fabric for flowers
- ¼ yard of green fabric for stems and calyxes*
- 2 strips, 3" x 22", of green fabric for leaves*
- 8" x 8" piece of thin, dense batting
- Sewing thread to match fabrics
- Small piece of template material
- 1 yard of green embellishing thread

These green fabrics may be the same.

Making the Quilt Top

UNLIKE A standard appliqué quilt, this project requires that you quilt and bind the quilt top before adding the appliquéd flowers. Work through the following steps, referring to "Basic Quilt Construction" (page 10) as needed.

1. Layer the backing, batting, and background squares.

2. Baste and quilt the layers, and then square the quilt to 6" x 6".

3. Use the 2½" x 42" strip of golden yellow fabric to make the binding and finish the edges of the quilt.

Making the Flowers

1. Referring to "Making Basic Flower Petals" (page 14), use the 2" x 22" strips of yellow fabric to make 33 petals as shown. Each petal shape should measure about ⅜" wide at the bottom and 1" long. Cut out the petals, trimming close to the stitching at the top of the petal to reduce the bulk. Turn the petals right side out. Use caution when pushing out the tops of the petals; it's easy to push through the seam at the top. Finger-press the petals into shape.

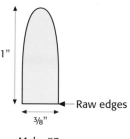

Make 33.

2. Thread a hand-sewing needle with thread to match the yellow fabric. Join five petals, pulling the thread to gather the petals slightly. Go through the petals several times to lock the flower shape into a ring; knot the thread. Make six flowers. Join the remaining three petals, pulling the thread tightly to gather the petals into a small bud.

Make 6.   Make 1.

3. Use the pattern on page 32 to make a star flower center template. Referring to "Making Yo-Yos" (page 22), use the template to cut six circles, 1⅛" in diameter, from the remainder of the 2½"-wide strip of golden yellow binding fabric. Make six tightly gathered basic yo-yos. Blind stitch a yo-yo to the center of each flower, making sure all raw edges of the

flower are covered by the yo-yo. (You will not stitch a yo-yo to the bud.) Knot the thread on the back of the flower.

Making the Leaves, Stems, and Calyx

1. Referring to "Making Bias Tape" (page 18), use the green stem fabric to make 36" of ¼"-wide bias tape. Fold the strips in half to measure ⅛" wide; press. Refer to the quilt photo on page 30 and cut the strips into seven stems of varying lengths. Appliqué the stems to the prepared background, making sure your stitches don't go through to the backing fabric.

2. Referring to "Making Basic Leaves" (page 19), use the two 3" x 22" strips of green leaf fabric to make five leaves as shown. Each leaf shape should measure about ½" wide at the bottom and 1½" long. Cut out the leaves and turn them right side out, finger-pressing them into shape. Turn up a ⅛" hem around the bottom of each leaf and finger-press. Use matching green thread to tightly gather the bottom of each leaf. Refer to the quilt photo and appliqué the bottom edge of each leaf to the base of the flower stems.

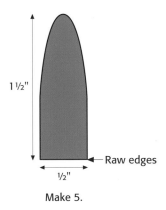

1½"

½"

← Raw edges

Make 5.

3. Referring to "Making Hump-Shaped Petals" (page 16), use the remaining green stem fabric to make one ¾" x ¾" hump shape to use as a calyx on the flower bud. Cut out the calyx and turn it right side out. Finger-press a ⅛" hem around the bottom of the calyx. Insert the three-petal bud into the calyx, making sure all raw edges of the bud are covered. Using matching green thread, blind stitch the calyx to the bud, pulling the thread slightly to gather.

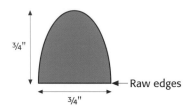

¾"

¾"

← Raw edges

Finishing

Refer to the quilt photo on page 30 as needed.

1. Appliqué the six flowers and the flower bud to the tops of the stems.

2. Referring to "Couching Threads for Embellishment" (page 23), couch the green embellishing thread along the bottom of the stems to form the grass.

Star flower center
Cut 6.

GOLDEN STAR FLOWERS

Embellishing threads and beads make this flower a shining star.

FINISHED SIZE: 6½" x 11½"

Materials

Materials are based on fabric that measures 42" wide.

- 2 pieces, 8½" x 13½", of mottled blue fabric for background and backing
- 1 strip, 2½" x 42", of golden yellow fabric for binding
- 2 strips, 3" x 22", of golden yellow fabric for flowers
- 2 strips, 3" x 22", of green fabric for leaves*
- ¼ yard of green fabric for stems*
- 8½" x 13½" piece of thin, dense batting
- Sewing thread to match fabrics
- 3½ yards of orange yarn for embellishing
- Water-soluble fabric glue
- 21 black seed beads

These green fabrics may be the same.

Making the Quilt Top

UNLIKE A standard appliqué quilt, this project requires that you quilt and bind the quilt top before adding the appliquéd flowers. Work through the following steps, referring to "Basic Quilt Construction" (page 10) as needed.

1. Layer the backing, batting, and background squares.

2. Baste and quilt the layers, and then square the quilt to 6½" x 11½".

3. Use the 2½" x 42" strip of golden yellow fabric to make the binding and finish the edges of the quilt.

Making the Flowers

1. Referring to "Making Basic Flower Petals" (page 14), use the 3" x 22" strips of golden yellow fabric to make 35 petals as shown. Each petal shape should measure about ¾" wide at the bottom and 1½" long. Cut out the petals, trimming close to the stitching at the top of the petal to reduce the bulk. Turn the petals right side out. Use caution when pushing out the tops of the petals; it's easy to push through the seam at the top. Finger-press the petals into shape.

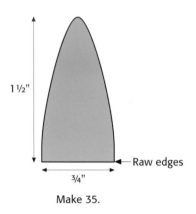

1½"

¾"

Raw edges

Make 35.

2. Thread a hand-sewing needle with thread to match the golden yellow fabric. Use a running stitch to join five petals, pulling the thread to gather the petals slightly. Go through the petals several times to lock the flowers into a loop; knot the thread. Make seven flowers.

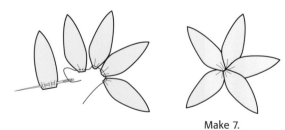

Make 7.

3. Cut the embellishing yarn into seven 18"-long pieces. Wrap one piece of embellishing yarn around your finger 8 to 10 times, and then twist the loops into a figure-eight shape. Thread a hand-sewing needle with thread to match the yarn. Place the twisted loop of yarn on the center of a flower and stab stitch the center of the loop down to cover the flower center. Repeat for each flower.

4. Use a stab stitch to sew three black seed beads in the center of each flower; knot the thread on the back of the flower.

Making the Leaves and Stems

1. Referring to "Making Basic Leaves" (page 19), use the two 3" x 22" strips of green leaf fabric to make 12 leaves as shown. Each leaf shape should measure ¾" wide at the bottom and 1½" long. Cut out the leaves and turn them right side out, finger-pressing them into shape. Use matching green thread to tightly gather the bottom of each leaf.

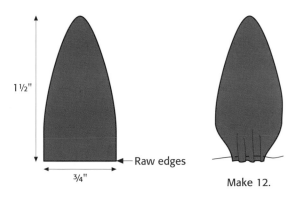

Make 12.

2. Referring to "Making Bias Tape" (page 18), use the green stem fabric to make 36" of ¼"-wide bias tape. Refer to the quilt photo on page 33 and cut the strips into seven stems of varying lengths. Glue-baste the stems to the prepared background fabric, tucking the leaves from step 1 behind the stems. Make sure the raw edges of the leaves are covered by the stems.

3. Appliqué the stems in place, stitching through the leaves to attach them to the background.

Finishing

Refer to the quilt photo on page 33 as needed. Appliqué the seven flowers to the tops of the stems.

DAFFODILS 1

When daffodils show their sunny faces, you know that spring is not far behind.
Daffodils come in many shades of yellow, orange, and white. If you change the color of the petals
or the cup, you can create endless variations.

FINISHED SIZE: 8½" x 7"

Materials

Materials are based on fabric that measures 42" wide.

- 2 pieces, 9" x 10½", of green batik fabric for background and backing
- 2 strips, 3" x 22", of sunny yellow fabric for flower petals
- 1 strip, 2" x 22", of golden yellow fabric for flower center cups
- 2 strips, 5" x 11", of green fabric for leaves*
- ¼ yard of green fabric for stems and calyxes*
- 1 strip, 2½" x 42", of golden yellow fabric for binding
- 9" x 10½" piece of thin, dense batting
- Sewing thread to match fabrics
- Water-soluble fabric glue

These green fabrics may be the same.

Making the Quilt Top

UNLIKE A standard appliqué quilt, this project requires that you quilt the quilt top before adding the appliquéd flowers. Work through the following steps, referring to "Basic Quilt Construction" (page 10) as needed.

1. Layer the backing, batting, and background squares.

2. Baste and quilt the layers, and then square the quilt to 8½" x 7". Don't bind the quilt yet.

Making the Flowers

1. Referring to "Making Basic Flower Petals" (page 14), use the 3" x 22" strips of yellow fabric to make 42 petals as shown. Each petal shape should measure about ⅜" wide at the bottom and 1½" long. Cut out the petals, trimming close to the stitching at the top of the petal to reduce the bulk. Turn the petals right side out. Use caution when pushing out the tops of the petals; it's easy to push through the seam at the top. Finger-press the petals into shape.

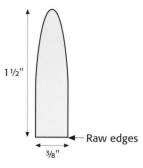

Make 42.

2. Thread a hand-sewing needle with thread to match the yellow fabric. Join six petals, pulling the thread to gather the petals slightly. Go through the petals several times to lock the flower shape into a ring; knot the thread. Make seven flowers.

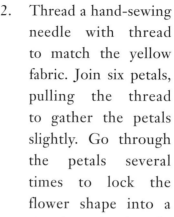

Make 7.

3. Fold a ¼"-wide hem down both long sides of the 2" x 22" strip of golden yellow fabric; press. Fold the strip in half lengthwise with wrong sides together; press. The strip should now measure ¾" x 22".

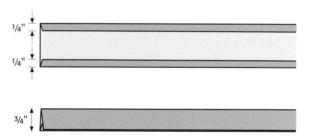

4. Cut the strip into seven 3"-long sections. Turn under a ¼" hem on one end of each section; press. With right sides out, loop the raw edge of each strip around and into the finished edge of the strip. Use matching-colored thread to blind stitch the seam.

Fold under ¼" hem.

Tuck raw edge into finished edge.

Make 7.

5. Use a running stitch to gather the top folded edge of each strip slightly; knot the thread. Use a running stitch to gather the bottom edge of each strip tightly to form a cup shape. Pass the needle through the bottom edge several times to lock the shape; knot the thread.

Gather top slightly. Gather bottom tightly.

6. Use matching-colored thread to blind stitch a cup to the center of each flower, making sure to cover all raw edges of the flower. Knot the thread on the back of the flower. Make seven.

Make 7.

Making the Leaves, Stems, and Calyxes

1. Referring to "Making Basic Leaves" (page 19), use the two 5" x 11" strips of green leaf fabric to make five leaves as shown. (You will not need to crease the strip and will stitch across its entire width.) Each leaf shape should measure about ½" wide at the bottom and 4¾" long. Cut out the leaves and turn them right side out, finger-pressing them into shape.

4¾"

← Raw edges

½"

Make 5.

2. Referring to "Making Bias Tape" (page 18), use the green stem fabric to make 36" of ¼"-wide bias tape. Refer to the quilt photo on page 36 and cut the strips into seven stems of varying lengths. Glue-baste the stems to the prepared background fabric, aligning the raw edge of the stem with the raw edge of the quilt. Glue-baste the bottom of the leaves to the bottom edge of the quilt, aligning the raw edges.

3. Refer to the quilt photo and appliqué the stems to the background. Fold the leaves down and tack in place.

4. Referring to "Binding the Quilt" (page 12), use the 2½" x 42" strip of golden yellow fabric to make the binding and finish the edges of the quilt. Make sure the raw edges of the leaves and stems are covered by the binding.

5. Referring to "Making Hump-Shaped Petals" (page 16), use the remaining green stem fabric to make two ¾" x ¾" hump shapes to use as calyxes for two of the flowers. Cut out the calyxes and turn them right side out. Finger-press a ⅛" hem around the bottom of each calyx. Insert a flower into each calyx to make a bud, making sure all raw edges of the bud are covered. Using matching green thread, blind stitch the calyx to the bud, pulling the thread slightly to gather. Make two buds.

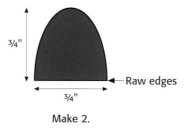

¾"

¾"

← Raw edges

Make 2.

Finishing

REFER TO the quilt photo on page 36 as needed. Appliqué the five flowers and the two buds to the tops of the stems.

DAFFODILS 2

Daffodils mark the end of winter. Like a ray of sunshine, they warm our hearts with the promise of spring.

FINISHED SIZE: 6" x 10"

Materials

Materials are based on fabric that measures 42" wide.

- 2 pieces, 8" x 12", of sky blue fabric for background and backing
- 2 strips, 3" x 22", of yellow fabric for flower petals
- 1 strip, 2" x 22", of yellow fabric for flower center cups
- 2 strips, 5" x 11", of green fabric for leaves*
- ¼ yard of green fabric for stems and calyxes*
- 1 strip, 2½" x 42", of yellow fabric for binding
- 8" x 12" piece of thin, dense batting
- Sewing thread to match fabrics
- Water-soluble fabric glue
- 2 yards of green embellishing thread for grass

These green fabrics may be the same.

Making the Quilt Top

UNLIKE A standard appliqué quilt, this project requires that you quilt the quilt top before adding the appliquéd flowers. Work through the following steps, referring to "Basic Quilt Construction" (page 10) as needed.

1. Layer the backing, batting, and background squares.

2. Baste and quilt the layers, and then square the quilt to 6" x 10". Don't bind the quilt yet.

Making the Flowers

1. Referring to "Making Basic Flower Petals" (page 14), use the 3" x 22" strips of yellow fabric to make 42 petals as shown. Each petal shape should measure about ⅜" wide at the bottom and 1½" long. Cut out the petals, trimming close to the stitching at the top of the petal to reduce the bulk. Turn the petals

right side out. Use caution when pushing out the tops of the petals; it's easy to push through the seam at the top. Finger-press the petals into shape.

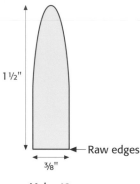

1½"

⅜"

Raw edges

Make 42.

2. Thread a hand-sewing needle with thread to match the yellow fabric. Use a running stitch to join six petals, pulling the thread to gather the petals slightly. Go through the petals several times to lock the flower shape into a ring; knot the thread. Make seven flowers.

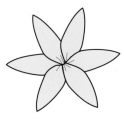

Make 7.

3. Fold a ¼"-wide hem down both long sides of the 2" x 22" strip of yellow fabric; press. Fold the strip in half lengthwise with wrong sides together; press. The strip should now measure ¾" x 22".

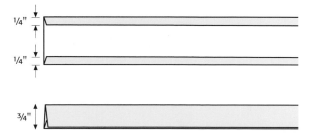

¼"

¼"

¾"

4. Cut the strip into seven 3"-long sections. Turn under a ¼" hem on one end of each section; press. With right sides out, loop the raw edge of each strip around and into the finished edge of the strip. Use matching-colored thread to blind stitch the seam.

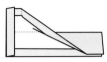

Fold under ¼" hem.　　Tuck raw edge into finished edge.　　Make 7.

5. Use a running stitch to gather the bottom edge of each strip tightly to form a cup shape. Pass the needle through the bottom edge several times to lock the shape; knot the thread.

Gather bottom tightly.

6. Use matching-colored thread to blind stitch a cup to the center of each flower, making sure to cover all raw edges of the flower. Knot the thread on the back of the flower. Make seven.

Make 7.

Making the Leaves, Stems, and Calyxes

1. Referring to "Making Basic Leaves" (page 19), use the two 5" x 11" strips of green leaf fabric to make three leaves as shown. (You will not need to crease the strip and will stitch across its entire width.) Each leaf shape should measure about ½" wide at the bottom and 4¾" long. Cut out the leaves and turn them right side out, finger-pressing them into shape.

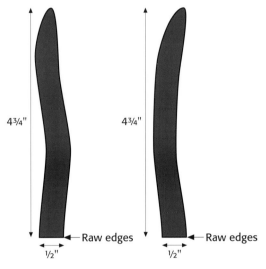

4¾"　　4¾"

← Raw edges　　← Raw edges

½"　　½"

Make 3 total

2. Referring to "Making Bias Tape" (page 18), use the green stem fabric to make 36" of ¼"-wide bias tape. Refer to the quilt photo on page 39 and cut the strips into five stems of varying lengths. Glue-baste the stems to the prepared background fabric, aligning the raw edge of the stem with the raw edge of the quilt. Glue-baste the bottom of the leaves to the bottom edge of the quilt, aligning the raw edges.

3. Refer to the quilt photo and appliqué the stems to the background. Fold the leaves down and tack in place.

4. Referring to "Binding the Quilt" (page 12), use the 2½" x 42" strip of yellow fabric to make the binding and finish the edges of the quilt. Make sure the raw edges of the leaves and stems are covered by the binding.

5. Referring to "Making Hump-Shaped Petals" (page 16), use the remaining green stem fabric to make two ¾" x ¾" hump shapes to use as calyxes for two of the flowers. Cut out the calyxes and turn them right side out. Finger-press a ⅛" hem around the bottom of each calyx. Insert a flower into each calyx to make a bud, making sure all raw edges of the bud are covered. Using matching green thread, blind stitch the calyx to the bud, pulling the thread slightly to gather. Make two buds.

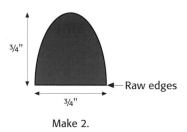

Make 2.

Finishing

REFER TO the quilt photo on page 39 as needed.

1. Appliqué the five flowers and two buds to the tops of the stems.

2. Referring to "Couching Threads for Embellishment" (page 23), couch the green embellishing thread along the bottom of the stems to form the grass, leaving the ends of the embellishing threads to dangle for added texture.

GOLDEN CONEFLOWERS

The golden coneflower is one of my favorite flowers.
I love the way the center demands to be seen, pushing the petals
downward to expose the flower's beauty to the world.

FINISHED SIZE: 8" x 5½"

Materials

Materials are based on fabric that measures 42" wide.

- 2 pieces, 7½" x 10", of sky blue fabric for background and backing
- 1 strip, 2½" x 42", of golden yellow fabric for binding
- 2 strips, 2" x 22", of yellow fabric for flower petals
- 2 strips, 2" x 11", of golden yellow fabric for flower centers
- ¼ yard of green fabric for stems*
- 2 strips, 4" x 11", of green fabric for leaves*
- 7½" x 10" piece of thin, dense batting
- Sewing thread to match fabrics
- 84 black seed beads

These green fabrics may be the same.

Making the Quilt Top

UNLIKE A standard appliqué quilt, this project requires that you quilt and bind the quilt top before adding the appliquéd flowers. Work through the following steps, referring to "Basic Quilt Construction" (page 10) as needed.

1. Layer the backing, batting, and background squares.

2. Baste and quilt the layers, and then square the quilt to 8" x 5½".

3. Use the 2½" x 42" strip of golden yellow fabric to make the binding and finish the edges of the quilt.

Making the Flowers

1. Referring to "Making Basic Flower Petals" (page 14), use the 2" x 22" strips of yellow fabric to make 35 petals as shown. Each petal shape should measure about ⅜" wide at the bottom and 1" long. Cut out the petals, trimming close to the stitching at the top of the

petal to reduce the bulk. Turn the petals right side out. Use caution when pushing out the tops of the petals; it's easy to push through the seam at the top. Finger-press the petals into shape.

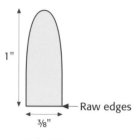

Make 35.

2. Thread a hand-sewing needle with thread to match the yellow fabric. Use a running stitch to join five petals. Don't join the petals into a ring; instead, reverse direction and go back through the five petals. Pull the thread gently to gather the petals into a fan shape; knot the thread. Make seven flowers.

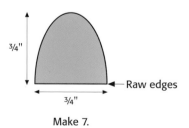

Make 7.

3. Referring to "Making Hump-Shaped Petals" (page 16), use the 2" x 11" strips of golden yellow fabric to make seven ¾" x ¾" hump shapes for the flower centers. Cut out the flower centers and turn them right side out. Finger-press a ⅛" hem around the bottom of each flower center.

Make 7.

4. Insert a flower from step 2 into a flower center from step 3, making sure all raw edges of the flower are covered. Using matching golden yellow thread, blind stitch the center to the flower, pulling the thread slightly to gather.

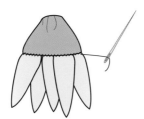

5. Stitch a row of 12 black seed beads around the bottom of each flower center. You can add the beads individually, or string them and couch them in place. Refer to "Beading" (page 22).

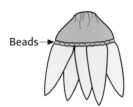

Making the Leaves and Stems

1. Referring to "Making Bias Tape" (page 18), use the green stem fabric to make 36" of ¼"-wide bias tape. Fold the bias tape in half to measure ⅛" wide; press. Refer to the quilt photo on page 43 and cut the strips into seven stems of varying lengths. Appliqué the stems to the prepared background, making sure your stitches don't go through to the backing fabric.

2. Referring to "Making Basic Leaves" (page 19), use the two 4" x 11" strips of green leaf fabric to make eight leaves as shown. Each leaf shape should measure about ⅜" wide at the bottom and vary from 1" to 2" long. Cut out the leaves and turn them right side out, finger-pressing them into shape. Turn up a ⅛" hem around the bottom of each leaf and finger-press. Use matching green thread to tightly gather the bottom of each leaf. Refer to the quilt photo and appliqué the leaves to the flower stems.

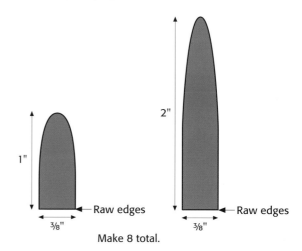

Make 8 total.

Finishing

REFER TO the quilt photo on page 43 as needed. Appliqué the seven flowers to the tops of the stems.

PURPLE SNOWDROPS

Snowdrop flowers come in many colors and are a welcome sign of spring.
They are one of the first flowers to bloom, often poking their heads up through the snow.

FINISHED SIZE: 9½" x 6"

Materials

Materials are based on fabric that measures 42" wide.

- ◆ 2 pieces, 8" x 11½", of yellow batik fabric for background and backing
- ◆ 1 strip, 3" x 22", of dark purple fabric for outer flower petals
- ◆ 1 strip, 3" x 22", of light purple fabric for inner flower petals
- ◆ 2 strips, 3" x 22", of green mottled fabric for leaves and calyxes*
- ◆ ¼ yard of green fabric for stems
- ◆ 1 strip, 2½" x 42", of dark purple fabric for binding
- ◆ 8" x 11" piece of thin, dense batting
- ◆ Sewing thread to match fabrics
- ◆ 1 yard of dark purple embellishing thread for flower stamens
- ◆ ¾ yard of yellow embellishing thread for flower stamens
- ◆ ⅓ yard of green embellishing thread for grass
- ◆ 16 purple beads
- ◆ 8 yellow beads
- ◆ Embellishing glue**
- ◆ Water-soluble fabric glue

This fabric may match the green fabric for stems.

**This product is often used for working with beads and jewelry. You can usually find it in bead and craft shops.*

Making the Quilt Top

UNLIKE a standard appliqué quilt, this project requires that you quilt the quilt top before adding the appliquéd flowers. Work through the following steps, referring to "Basic Quilt Construction" (page 10) as needed.

1. Layer the backing, batting, and background squares.

2. Baste and quilt the layers, and then square the quilt to 9½" x 6". Don't bind the quilt yet.

Making the Flowers

1. Referring to "Making Basic Flower Petals" (page 14), layer the 3" x 22" strips of light purple and dark purple fabric right sides together to make 24 petals as shown. Each petal shape should measure about ½" wide at the bottom and 1½" long. Cut out the petals, trimming close to the stitching at the top of the petal to reduce the bulk. Turn the petals right side out. Use caution when pushing out the tops of the petals; it's easy to push through the seam at the top. Finger-press the petals into shape.

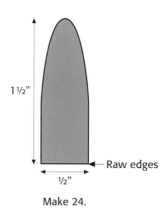

1½"

½"

Raw edges

Make 24.

2. Cut the purple embellishing thread into eight 3"-long pieces. Use embellishing glue to attach a purple bead to both ends of each piece of purple embellishing thread; allow the glue to dry. Cut the yellow embellishing thread into eight 2½"-long pieces. Use embellishing glue to attach a yellow bead to one end of each piece of yellow embellishing thread; allow the glue to dry.

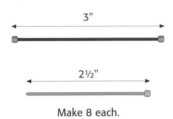

3"

2½"

Make 8 each.

3. Fold each purple thread from step 2 in half to find the center; crease the fold. Tightly knot a yellow thread to the center of each purple thread. Line up the three threads so the yellow thread is in the middle.

4. Thread a hand-sewing needle with thread to match the dark purple fabric. Use a running stitch to join three petals with the dark purple fabric on the outside. Insert a thread unit from step 3 in the center of the flower and pull the thread tightly to gather the petals. Stitch through the petals and the knot in the embellishing thread several times to lock the

flower shape into a ring; knot the thread. Make eight flowers.

Make 8.

Making the Leaves, Stems, and Calyxes

1. Referring to "Making Basic Leaves" (page 19), use the two 3" x 22" strips of green leaf fabric to make seven leaves, varying the sizes and shapes as shown. (You will not need to crease the strip and will stitch across its entire width.) Cut out the leaves and turn them right side out, finger-pressing them into shape.

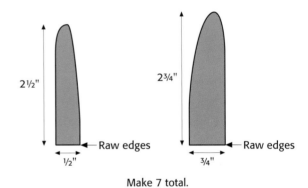

2½" 2¾"

Raw edges ← | → Raw edges

½" ¾"

Make 7 total.

2. Referring to "Making Bias Tape" (page 18), use the green stem fabric to make 36" of ¼"-wide bias tape. Refer to the quilt photo on page 46 and cut the strips into eight stems of varying lengths. Glue-baste the stems to the prepared background fabric, aligning the raw edge of the stem with the raw edge of the quilt. Glue-baste the bottom of the leaves to the bottom edge of the quilt, aligning the raw edges.

3. Appliqué the stems to the background. Twist and fold the leaves down and tack in place.

4. Referring to "Binding the Quilt" (page 12), use the 2½" x 42" strip of dark purple fabric to make the binding and finish the edges of the quilt. Make sure the raw edges of the leaves and stems are covered by the binding.

5. Referring to "Making Hump-Shaped Petals" (page 16), use the remaining green leaf fabric to make eight hump shapes to use as calyxes for the flowers. Each calyx shape should measure about ½" wide at the bottom and ¾" long. Cut out the calyxes and turn them right side out. Finger-press a ⅛" hem around the bottom of each calyx. Insert a flower into each calyx, making sure all raw edges of the flower are covered. Using matching green thread, blind stitch the calyx to the flower, pulling the thread slightly to gather. Stitch through the flower several times to lock the shape; knot the thread on the back of the flower. Make eight flowers.

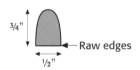

Make 8.

Finishing

REFER TO the quilt photo on page 46 as needed.

1. Appliqué the eight flowers to the tops of the stems.

2. Referring to "Couching Threads for Embellishment" (page 23), couch the green embellishing thread along the bottom of the stems to form the grass, leaving the ends of the embellishing threads to dangle for added texture.

SUNFLOWERS

The sunflower reminds me of hot August nights and sunny days.
Brighten up a friend's day with a bouquet of sunny sunflowers.

FINISHED SIZE: 8" x 13"

Materials

Materials are based on fabric that measures 42" wide.

- 2 pieces, 10" x 15", of sky blue fabric for background and backing
- 2 strips, 2½" x 42", of yellowish orange batik fabric for binding
- 4 strips, 3½" x 22", of yellowish orange batik fabric for flowers
- 1 strip, 3" x 9", of brown fabric for yo-yo flower centers
- 2 strips, 4" x 22", of green fabric for leaves*
- ¼ yard of green fabric for stems*
- 10" x 15" piece of thin, dense batting
- Sewing thread to match fabrics
- Small piece of template material
- 2" x 6" batting scrap for yo-yo flower centers
- 48 (approximately) black seed beads

These green fabrics may be the same.

Making the Quilt Top

UNLIKE A standard appliqué quilt, this project requires that you quilt and bind the quilt top before adding the appliquéd flowers. Work through the following steps, referring to "Basic Quilt Construction" (page 10) as needed.

1. Layer the backing, batting, and background squares.

2. Baste and quilt the layers, and then square the quilt to 8" x 13".

3. Use the 2½" x 42" strip of yellowish orange batik to make the binding and finish the edges of the quilt.

Making the Flowers

1. Referring to "Making Basic Flower Petals" (page 14), use the 3½" x 22" strips of yellowish orange batik to make two strip sets. Use the strip sets to make 44 petals as shown. Each petal shape should measure about 1" wide at the bottom and 1¾" long. Cut out the petals, trimming close to the stitching at the top of the petal to reduce the bulk. Turn the petals right side out. Use caution when pushing out the tops of the petals; it's easy to push through the seam at the top. Finger-press the petals into shape.

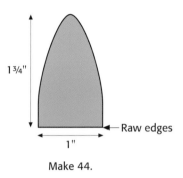

1¾"

1"

Raw edges

Make 44.

2. Thread a hand-sewing needle with thread to match the yellowish orange fabric. Join 15 petals, pulling the thread slightly to gather the petals into a ring. There will be a large gap in the center. Use your fingers to evenly distribute the gathers; knot the thread. Make one flower with 15 petals, one flower with 17 petals, and one flower with 12 petals.

Make 1 with 15 petals,
1 with 17 petals,
and 1 with 12 petals.

3. Use the pattern on page 53 to make a sunflower center (fabric) template. Use the template to cut three circles, 3" in diameter, from the 3" x 9" strip of brown fabric.

4. Referring to "Making Yo-Yos" (page 22), make three raw-edged yo-yos. Gather the yo-yos slightly; don't knot or cut the thread.

5. Use the pattern on page 53 to make a sunflower center (batting) template. Use the template to cut three circles, 2" in diameter, from the 2" x 6" batting scrap.

6. Insert a 2" batting circle into each yo-yo from step 4. Pull the thread to gather the yo-yo around the batting; knot the thread. With raw edges down, blind stitch a yo-yo to the center of each flower, making sure all raw edges of the flower are covered by the yo-yo. Knot the thread on the back of the flower.

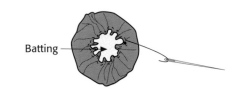

7. Stitch a ring of approximately 15 black seed beads to each flower center, about ½" from the edge as shown. You can add the beads individually, or string them and then couch them in place. Refer to "Beading" (page 22). Pull the thread to nestle the beads into the batting. Finish by stitching one bead with a stab stitch in the center of each flower. Knot the thread on the back of the flower.

Making the Leaves and Stems

1. Referring to "Making Bias Tape" (page 18), use the green stem fabric to make 36" of ⅜"-wide bias tape. Refer to the quilt photo on page 50 and cut the strips into three stems of varying lengths. Appliqué the stems to the prepared background, making sure your stitches don't go through to the backing fabric.

2. Use the pattern on page 53 to make a leaf template. Referring to "Making Basic Leaves" (page 19), use the template to trace five leaves on the 4" x 22" strips of green leaf fabric. Use matching green thread to machine stitch around each leaf shape; leave an opening for turning as shown in the diagram on page 53 and on the pattern.

3. Cut out the leaves. Clip the inside curve at the top of the leaf shapes and turn them right side out, finger-pressing them into shape. Tuck the raw edges into the opening on each leaf and finger-press. Use matching green thread to topstitch around the outside of each leaf, making sure to stitch the opening closed. Stitch the center vein.

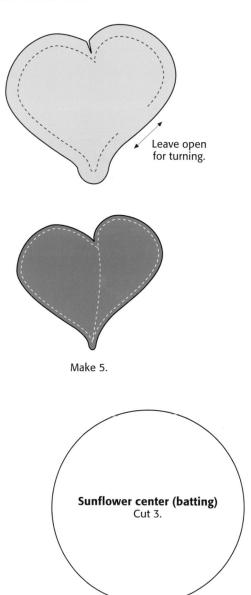

Leave open for turning.

Make 5.

Finishing

REFER TO the quilt photo on page 50 as needed. Tack the five leaves and appliqué the three flowers to the stems.

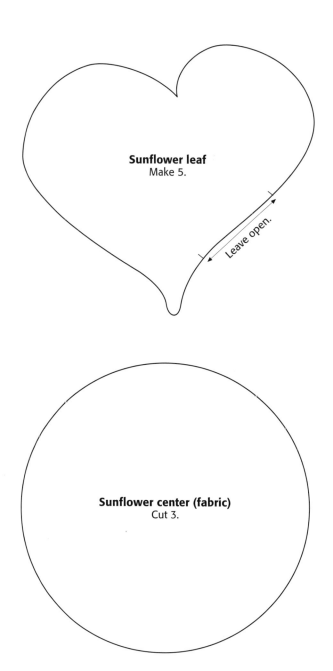

Sunflower leaf
Make 5.

Leave open.

Sunflower center (batting)
Cut 3.

Sunflower center (fabric)
Cut 3.

POINSETTIAS

Poinsettias remind me of the holidays, spending time with loved ones, and good food.
This project makes a perfect gift for someone you love.

FINISHED SIZE: 12½" x 16"

Materials

Materials are based on fabric that measures 42" wide.

- 2 pieces, 14½" x 18", of cream fabric for background and backing
- 2 strips, 2½" x 42", of mottled red fabric for binding
- 4 strips, 5" x 22", of mottled red fabric for large flower petals
- 4 strips, 3" x 22", of mottled red fabric for medium flower petals
- 2 strips, 2½" x 22", of mottled red fabric for small flower petals
- 2 strips, 3½" x 22", of green fabric for leaves
- 14½" x 18" piece of thin, dense batting
- 2½ yards of gold embellishing thread
- Sewing thread to match fabrics
- 96 (approximately) gold-lined green beads

Making the Quilt Top

UNLIKE A standard appliqué quilt, this project requires that you quilt and bind the quilt top before adding the appliquéd flowers. Work through the following steps, referring to "Basic Quilt Construction" (page 10) as needed.

1. Layer the backing, batting, and background squares.

2. Baste and quilt the layers, and then square the quilt to 12½" x 16".

3. Referring to "Couching Threads for Embellishment" on page 23 and the quilt photo on page 54, machine stitch the gold embellishing thread to the background.

4. Use the 2½" x 42" strips of mottled red fabric to make the binding and finish the edges of the quilt.

Making the Flowers

1. Referring to "Making Basic Flower Petals" (page 14), use the 5" x 22" strips of red fabric to make two strip sets. Use the strip sets to make 56 petals as shown. Each petal shape should measure about ¾" wide at the bottom and 2½" long. Cut out the petals, trimming close to the stitching at the top of the petal to reduce the bulk. Turn the petals right side out. Use caution when pushing out the tops of the petals; it's easy to push through the seam at the top. Finger-press the petals into shape.

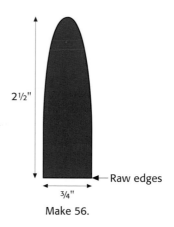

2½"

¾"

◄— Raw edges

Make 56.

2. Thread a hand-sewing needle with thread to match the red fabric. Use a running stitch to join seven petals, pulling the thread to gather the petals slightly. Go through the petals several times to lock the flower shape into a ring; knot the thread. Make eight large flowers.

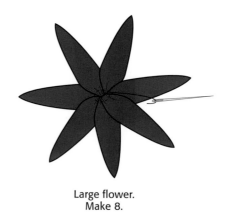

Large flower.
Make 8.

3. Repeat step 1, using the 3" x 22" strips of red fabric to make 48 petals. Each petal shape should measure about ½" wide at the bottom and 1½" long.

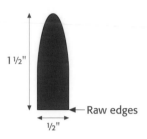

1½"

←— Raw edges

½"

Make 48.

4. Repeat step 2 to make eight medium flowers, each with six petals.

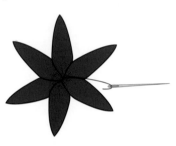

Medium flower.
Make 8.

5. Repeat step 1, using the 2½" x 22" strips of red fabric to make one strip set; make 40 petals. Each petal shape should measure about ⅜" wide at the bottom and 1¼" long.

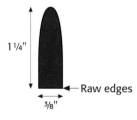

1¼"

←— Raw edges

⅜"

Make 40.

6. Repeat step 2 to make eight small flowers, each with five petals.

Small flower
Make 8.

7. Thread a hand-sewing needle with thread to match the red fabric. Layer one medium flower over a large flower, offsetting the petals. Stitch the two flowers together. Layer a small flower over the medium flower, once again offsetting the petals, and stitch through all three flowers to join them. Make eight flowers.

Make 8.

8. Thread a hand-sewing needle with thread to match the red fabric and stab stitch about 12 gold-lined green beads in a cluster at the center of each flower. Make sure the beads cover the raw edges at the center of the flower.

Making the Leaves

1. Referring to "Making Basic Leaves" (page 19), use the 3½" x 22" strips of green leaf fabric to make 30 leaves as shown. Each leaf shape should measure about ¾" wide at the bottom and 1¾" long. Cut out the leaves and turn them right side out, finger-pressing them into shape. Turn up a ⅛" hem around the bottom of each leaf and finger-press.

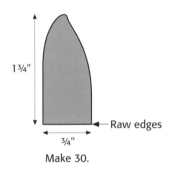

1¾"

← Raw edges

¾"

Make 30.

2. Thread a hand-sewing needle with thread to match the green fabric. Join two or three leaves together loosely; knot the thread. Make eight. Stitch a set of leaves to the back of each flower. (You will have some leaves left over.)

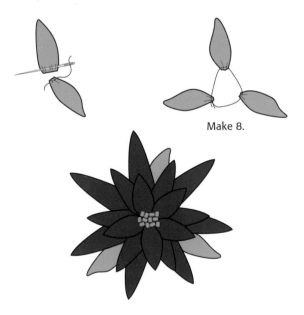

Make 8.

Finishing

REFER TO the quilt photo on page 54 as needed.

1. Appliqué the eight flowers to the background fabric.

2. Thread a hand-sewing needle with thread to match the green leaf fabric. Tightly gather the bottom of each remaining leaf and appliqué the leaves along the embellishing thread.

SIMPLE FIVE-PETAL FLOWERS

This project is very easy to make. I really like the elegance of the burgundy batik fabric combined with the black embellishing thread. You can make the flowers any color you like.

FINISHED SIZE: 6" x 13"

Materials

Materials are based on fabric that measures 42" wide.

- 2 pieces, 8" x 15", of cream fabric for background and backing
- 2 strips, 3" x 30", of burgundy batik fabric for flowers
- ¼ yard of green fabric for stems*
- 1 strip, 2½" x 42", of burgundy batik fabric for binding
- 2 strips, 3" x 22", of green fabric for leaves*
- 8" x 15" piece of thin, dense batting
- Sewing thread to match fabrics
- 3 yards of black embellishing thread
- 21 white beads for flower centers

These green fabrics may be the same.

Making the Quilt Top

UNLIKE A standard appliqué quilt, this project requires that you quilt the quilt top before adding the appliquéd flowers. Work through the following steps, referring to "Basic Quilt Construction" (page 10) as needed.

1. Layer the backing, batting, and background squares.

2. Baste and quilt the layers, and then square the quilt to 6" x 13". Don't bind the quilt yet.

Making the Flowers

1. Referring to "Making Hump-Shaped Petals" (page 16), use the 3" x 30" strips of burgundy batik fabric to make 35 petals. Each petal shape should measure about 1" wide at the bottom and 1¼" long. Cut out the petals, trimming close to the stitching at the top of the petal to reduce the bulk. Turn the petals right side out. Use caution when pushing out the tops of the petals; it's easy to push through the seam at the top. Finger-press the petals into shape.

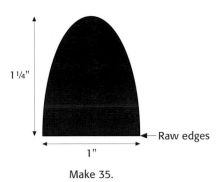

1¼"

1"

Raw edges

Make 35.

2. Thread a hand-sewing needle with thread to match the burgundy fabric. Use a running stitch to join five petals, pulling the thread to gather the petals slightly. Go through the petals several times to lock the flower shape into a ring; then knot the thread. Make seven flowers.

Make 7.

3. Cut the embellishing thread into seven 15"-long pieces. Wrap one piece of embellishing thread around your finger 8 to 10 times, and then twist the loops into a figure-eight shape.

4. Thread a hand-sewing needle with thread to match the embellishing thread. Place the twisted loop of embellishing thread on the center of one flower and stab stitch the center of the loop down to cover the flower center. Repeat for each flower.

5. Stab stitch three white beads in the center of each flower; knot the thread on the back of the flower.

Making the Leaves and Stems

1. Referring to "Making Bias Tape" (page 18), use the green stem fabric to make 60" of ¼"-wide bias tape. Refer to the quilt photo on page 58 and cut the strips into six stems of varying lengths. Glue-baste the stems to the prepared background fabric, aligning the raw edges of the stems with the raw edge of the quilt.

2. Appliqué the stems to the background fabric.

3. Referring to "Binding the Quilt" (page 12), use the 2½" x 42" strip of burgundy batik fabric to make the binding and finish the edges of the quilt. Make sure the raw edges of the stems are covered by the binding.

4. Referring to "Making Basic Leaves" (page 19), use the two 3" x 22" strips of green leaf fabric to make 12 leaves as shown. Each leaf shape should measure ¾" wide at the bottom and 1½" long. Cut out the leaves and turn them right side out, finger-pressing them into shape.

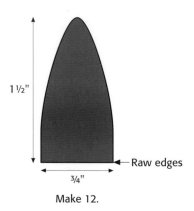

Make 12.

5. Use matching green thread to tightly gather the bottom of each leaf. Refer to the quilt photo and stitch two leaves to the back of five flowers and one leaf to each of the remaining two flowers; knot the thread.

Finishing

REFER TO the quilt photo on page 58 as needed. Appliqué the seven flowers to the stems.

PANSIES

The pansy is one of the happiest flowers in the garden. I love the way the petals form a smiling face. You'll love how easy this flower is to make.

FINISHED SIZE: 6" x 12"

Materials

Materials are based on fabric that measures 42" wide.

- 2 pieces, 8" x 14", of mottled purple fabric for background and backing
- 1 strip, 2½" x 42", of dark purple fabric for binding
- 2 strips, 3" x 15", of orange fabric for flowers
- 2 strips, 3" x 11", of dark purple fabric for flowers
- 2 strips, 4" x 11", of green fabric for leaves and calyxes
- ¼ yard of green fabric for stems
- 8" x 14" piece of thin, dense batting
- Sewing thread to match fabrics
- 5 small black bugle beads
- 10 green seed beads
- Water-soluble fabric glue

Making the Quilt Top

Unlike a standard appliqué quilt, this project requires that you quilt and bind the quilt top before adding the appliquéd flowers. Work through the following steps, referring to "Basic Quilt Construction" (page 10) as needed.

1. Layer the backing, batting, and background squares.

2. Baste and quilt the layers, and then square the quilt to 6" x 12".

3. Use the 2½" x 42" strip of dark purple fabric to make the binding and finish the edges of the quilt.

Making the Flowers

1. Referring to "Making Hump-Shaped Petals" (page 16), use the 3" x 15" strips of orange fabric to make 16 petals. Each petal shape should measure about 1¼" wide at the bottom and 1¼" long. Cut out the petals, trimming

close to the stitching at the top of the petal to reduce the bulk. Turn the petals right side out. Use caution when pushing out the tops of the petals; it's easy to push through the seam at the top. Finger-press the petals into shape.

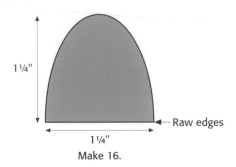

1¼"

1¼"

Raw edges

Make 16.

2. Use the 3" x 11" strips of dark purple fabric to make 12 hump-shaped petals the same size as the orange petals in step 1. Cut out the petals and turn them right side out. Finger-press the petals into shape.

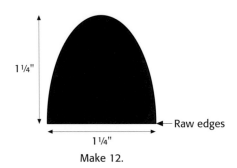

1¼"

1¼"

Raw edges

Make 12.

3. Thread a hand-sewing needle with thread to match the orange fabric. Use a running stitch to join three orange petals with two purple petals, pulling the thread to gather the petals slightly. Go through the petals several times to lock the flower shape into a ring; knot the thread. Make five flowers.

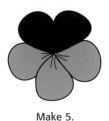

Make 5.

4. Thread a hand-sewing needle with thread to match the purple fabric and stab stitch one black bugle bead in the center of each flower. Stab stitch a green seed bead on opposite sides of the bugle bead; knot the thread.

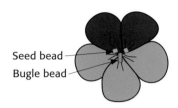

Seed bead
Bugle bead

5. Roll one remaining purple petal around one orange petal to make a bud and stitch to secure. Roll the remaining purple petal into a bud; stitch to secure.

Make 1 orange
wrapped in purple.

Make 1
purple.

Making the Leaves, Stems, and Calyxes

1. Referring to "Making Basic Leaves" (page 19), use the two 4" x 11" strips of green leaf fabric to make six leaves as shown. Each leaf shape should measure about ¾" wide at the bottom and 2" long. Cut out the leaves and turn them right side out, finger-pressing them into shape. Turn up a ⅛" hem around the bottom of three leaves and finger-press. Leave the bottom edges of the remaining three leaves unhemmed. Use matching green thread to tightly gather the bottom of each leaf.

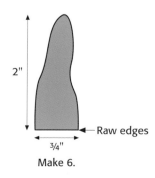

2"

¾"

Raw edges

Make 6.

2. Referring to "Making Bias Tape" (page 18), use the green stem fabric to make 36" of ¼"-wide bias tape. Refer to the quilt photo on page 61 and cut the strips into four stems of varying lengths. Glue-baste the stems to the prepared background fabric, tucking the three unhemmed leaves behind the stems to cover the raw edges.

3. Appliqué the stems and the three raw-edged leaves to the background.

4. Referring to "Making Hump-Shaped Petals" (page 16), use the remaining green leaf fabric to make two ¾" x ¾" hump shapes to use as calyxes for the two buds. Cut out the calyxes and turn them right side out. Finger-press a ⅛" hem around the bottom of each calyx. Insert a bud into each calyx, making sure all raw edges of the bud are covered. Using matching green thread, blind stitch the calyx to the bud, pulling the thread slightly to gather. Make two.

Make 2 buds.

Finishing

REFER TO the quilt photo on page 61 as needed.

1. Appliqué the five flowers and two buds to the stems.

2. Appliqué the three finished-edge leaves to the stems.

TWO-TONED FOLDED-PETAL FLOWERS

This flower is another quick and easy version of the five-petal flower (page 58).
Folding the petals gives the flower texture. Any color combination will work.
Try using a light fabric and a dark fabric for dramatic results.

FINISHED SIZE: 5" x 12"

Materials

Materials are based on fabric that measures 42" wide.

- 2 pieces, 7" x 14", of cream fabric for background and backing
- 1 strip, 2½" x 42", of green fabric for binding
- 1 strip, 3" x 22", of gold print for flowers
- 1 strip, 3" x 22", of gold tone-on-tone print for flowers
- 2 strips, 2½" x 22", of green fabric for leaves and calyx*
- ¼ yard of green fabric for stems*
- 7" x 14" piece of thin, dense batting
- Sewing thread to match fabrics
- 2 yards of pink embellishing thread
- 15 white beads
- Water-soluble fabric glue

* These green fabrics may be the same.

Making the Quilt Top

UNLIKE A standard appliqué quilt, this project requires that you quilt and bind the quilt top be-fore adding the appliquéd flowers. Work through the following steps, referring to "Basic Quilt Construction" (page 10) as needed.

1. Layer the backing, batting, and background squares.

2. Baste and quilt the layers, and then square the quilt to 5" x 12".

3. Use the 2½" x 42" strip of green fabric to make the binding and finish the edges of the quilt.

Making the Flowers

1. Referring to "Making Hump-Shaped Petals" (page 16), layer the 3" x 22" strips of gold print and gold tone-on-tone print right sides together to make 28 petals. Each petal shape should measure about 1" wide at the bottom

and 1¼" long. Cut out the petals, trimming close to the stitching at the top of the petal to reduce the bulk. Turn the petals right side out. Use caution when pushing out the tops of the petals; it's easy to push through the seam at the top. Finger-press the petals into shape.

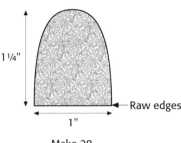

1¼"

1"

◄— Raw edges

Make 28.

2. Thread a hand-sewing needle with thread to match the gold fabrics. Fold a petal in half with the lighter color on the inside, and crease. Unfold the petal. Fold over one side of the petal, and then the other side to meet at the crease line; finger-press. Sew through all the layers of fabric with a running stitch at the base of the petal to secure the folds.

3. Use the same gold thread and a running stitch to join five petals, pulling the thread to gather the petals slightly. Go through the petals several times to lock the flower shape into a ring; knot the thread. Make five flowers. Join the remaining three petals tightly to make a bud.

Make 5.

Make 1.

4. Cut the embellishing thread into five 14"-long pieces. Wrap one piece of embellishing thread around your finger 8 to 10 times, and then twist the loops into a figure-eight shape. Thread a hand-sewing needle with thread to match the embellishing thread. Place the twisted loop of embellishing thread on the center of one flower and stab stitch the center of the loop down to cover the flower center. Repeat for each flower.

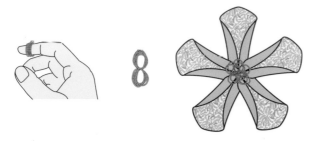

5. Stab stitch three white beads in the center of each flower; knot the thread on the back of the flower.

Making the Leaves, Stems, and Calyx

1. Referring to "Making Basic Leaves" (page 19), use the two 2½" x 22" strips of green leaf fabric to make 11 petal-shaped leaves. Each leaf shape should measure about ½" wide at the bottom and 1¼" long. Cut out the leaves

and turn them right side out, finger-pressing them into shape.

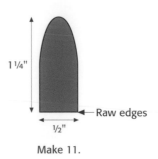

Make 11.

2. Referring to "Making Hump-Shaped Petals" (page 16), use the remaining green leaf fabric to make one ¾" x ¾" hump shape to use as a calyx for the flower bud. Cut out the calyx and turn it right side out. Finger-press a ⅛" hem around the bottom of the calyx. Insert the bud into the calyx, making sure all raw edges of the bud are covered. Using matching green thread, blind stitch the calyx to the bud, pulling the thread slightly to gather.

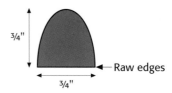

3. Referring to "Making Bias Tape" (page 18), use the green stem fabric to make 48" of ¼"-wide bias tape. Refer to the quilt photo on page 64 and cut the strips into five stems of varying lengths. Glue-baste the stems to the prepared background fabric, tucking the leaves behind the stems to cover the raw edges.

4. Appliqué the stems and leaves to the background.

Finishing

REFER TO the quilt photo on page 64 as needed. Appliqué the five flowers and the bud to the stems.

FUCHSIA

The fuchsia—a Mother's Day favorite—is considered a symbol of love.

FINISHED SIZE: 7" x 7"

Materials

Materials are based on fabric that measures 42" wide.

- 2 pieces, 9" x 9", of cream fabric for background and backing
- 1 strip, 3½" x 22", of purple batik fabric for flowers
- 1 strip, 3½" x 22", of yellow fabric for flowers
- 2 strips, 2" x 22", of green fabric for calyxes and leaves*
- ¼ yard of green fabric for stems*
- 1 strip, 2½" x 42", of purple batik fabric for binding
- 9" x 9" piece of thin, dense batting
- Sewing thread to match fabrics
- 4 yards of orange embellishing thread

These green fabrics may be the same.

Making the Quilt Top

UNLIKE A standard appliqué quilt, this project requires that you quilt the quilt top before adding the appliquéd flowers. Work through the following steps, referring to "Basic Quilt Construction" (page 10) as needed.

1. Layer the backing, batting, and background squares.

2. Baste and quilt the layers, and then square the quilt to 7" x 7". Don't bind the quilt yet.

Making the Flowers

1. Referring to "Making Hump-Shaped Petals" (page 16), layer the 3½" x 22" strips of purple batik and yellow fabric right sides together to make 29 petals. Each petal shape should measure about ¾" wide at the bottom and 1½" long. Cut out the petals, trimming close to the stitching at the top of the petal to reduce the bulk. Turn the petals right side

out. Use caution when pushing out the tops of the petals; it's easy to push through the seam at the top. Finger-press the petals into shape.

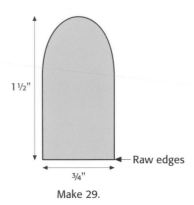

1½"

¾"

Raw edges

Make 29.

2. Cut the embellishing thread into eleven 13"-long pieces. Wrap a thread around two fingers four times. Knot the end of the thread to secure the loops as shown. Repeat with each piece of thread.

3. Thread a hand-sewing needle with thread to match the purple batik fabric. Use a running stitch to join three petals; pull the thread to gather the petals slightly. Make nine. Insert one thread unit from step 2 into the center of each flower as shown, making sure the knot is lined up with the raw edges of the petal. Pull the center of the flower closed more tightly and stitch through the petals and embellishing thread several times to lock the flower shape; knot the thread. Make nine flowers.

Make 9.

4. Roll a remaining flower petal around each remaining thread unit, pulling the thread to gather the petal slightly. Stitch through the petal and embellishing thread several times to lock the shape; knot the thread. Make two buds.

Make 2.

Making the Calyxes and Leaves

1. Referring to "Making Hump-Shaped Petals" (page 16), use the two 2" x 22" strips of green leaf fabric to make fifteen ¾" x ¾" hump shapes for calyxes and leaves. Cut out the shapes and turn them right side out.

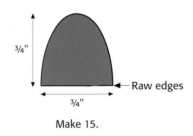

Make 15.

2. Finger-press a ⅛" hem around the bottom of each hump shape from step 1. Insert each flower or flower bud into a hump shape (calyx), making sure all raw edges of the flower or bud are covered. Using matching green thread, blind stitch the calyx to the flower or bud, pulling the thread slightly to gather. Stitch through the unit several times to lock the shape; knot the thread on the back. Make nine flowers and two buds.

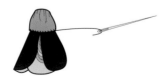

3. Use matching green thread to tightly gather the bottom of each remaining hump shape to make four leaves.

Making the Stems

1. Referring to "Making Bias Tape" (page 18), use the green stem fabric to make 36" of ¼"-wide bias tape. Refer to the quilt photo on page 67 and cut the strips into five stems of varying lengths. Glue-baste the stems to the prepared background fabric, aligning the raw edges of the stems with the raw edge of the quilt.

2. Appliqué the stems to the background fabric.

3. Referring to "Binding the Quilt" (page 12), use the 2½" x 42" strip of purple batik fabric to make the binding and finish the edges of the quilt. Make sure the raw edges of the stems are covered by the binding.

Finishing

REFER TO the quilt photo on page 67 as needed. Appliqué the nine flowers, two buds, and four leaves to the stems.

BLEEDING HEARTS

The bleeding heart is an old-fashioned flower that symbolizes love, home, and togetherness.
You can use this flower as filler in a fabric bouquet.

FINISHED SIZE: 10" x 6"

Materials

Materials are based on fabric that measures 42" wide.

- 2 pieces, 8" x 12", of light blue fabric for background and backing
- 1 strip, 2½" x 42", of pink batik fabric for binding
- 2 strips, 2½" x 22", of pink batik fabric for flowers
- 1 strip, 2" x 30", of white fabric for flower centers
- 2 strips, 2" x 22", of green fabric for leaves
- 8" x 12" piece of thin, dense batting
- Sewing thread to match fabrics
- 1 yard *each* of 2 different green embellishing threads for large and small stems

I used just one thread, a multi-ply chenille, for both stems. I used the entire thickness for the large stems and a single ply for the smaller stems that attach the flowers to the larger stems.

Making the Quilt Top

UNLIKE A standard appliqué quilt, this project requires that you quilt and bind the quilt top before adding the appliquéd flowers. Work through the following steps, referring to "Basic Quilt Construction" (page 10) as needed.

1. Layer the backing, batting, and background squares.

2. Baste and quilt the layers, and then square the quilt to 10" x 6".

3. Use the 2½" x 42" strip of pink batik fabric to make the binding and finish the edges of the quilt.

Making the Flowers

1. Referring to "Making Hump-Shaped Petals" (page 16), use the 2½" x 22" strips of pink batik fabric to make 20 petals. Each petal shape should vary from ¾" to 1" wide at the bottom and from ¾" to 1" long. Cut out the petals, trimming close to the stitching at the top of the petal to reduce the bulk. Turn the petals right side out. Use caution when pushing out the tops of the petals; it's easy to push through the seam at the top. Finger-press the petals into shape with the seams centered in the front and back of the petal.

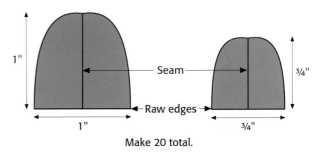

Make 20 total.

2. Finger-press a ⅛" hem around the bottom of each petal from step 1. Thread a hand-sewing needle with thread to match the fabric. Use a running stitch to gather the bottom of one petal; don't cut the thread. Instead, using the same thread, sew a running stitch all along the seam that joins the front and the back of the petal. Pull the thread to gather slightly; trim, leaving a 12" tail. Make 19.

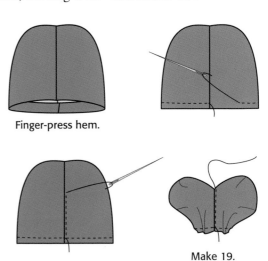

Finger-press hem.

Make 19.

3. Use a running stitch to tightly gather the bottom of the remaining petal; knot the thread. This petal will be used as a flower bud.

4. Cut the 2" x 30" strip of white fabric into nineteen 1½" x 2" pieces. Fold each piece of fabric in half with wrong sides together; finger-press. Fold the two upper corners inward as shown; finger-press.

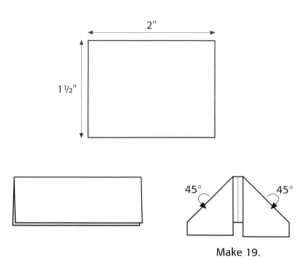

Make 19.

5. Roll each folded unit from step 4 into a tube to make a flower center as shown, tacking the bottom edge to secure. Insert a flower center into a flower from step 2, making sure the raw edges of the flower center are covered. Pull the unknotted sewing thread on the flower tightly to gather the flower into a heart shape around the flower center. Stitch through the unit several times to lock the flower shape; knot the thread on the back of the flower. Make 19 flowers.

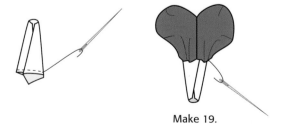

Make 19.

Making the Leaves

REFERRING TO "Making Basic Leaves" (page 19), use the two 2" x 22" strips of green leaf fabric to make 15 leaves as shown. Each leaf shape should measure about ¾" wide at the bottom and vary from ¾" to 1" in length. Cut out the leaves and turn them right side out, finger-pressing them into shape. Turn up a ⅛" hem around the bottom of each leaf and finger-press. Use matching green thread to tightly gather the bottom of each leaf.

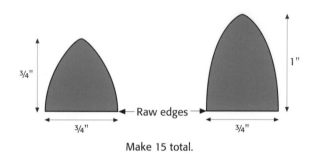

Make 15 total.

Finishing

REFER TO the quilt photo on page 70 as needed.

1. Referring to "Couching Threads for Embellishment" (page 23), couch the green embellishing thread to form the large and small stems.

2. Appliqué the 19 flowers, one bud, and 15 leaves to the stems.

Two-Color Bluebells

Although they are called bluebells, you can use any two colors for these flowers.

FINISHED SIZE: 6" x 7½"

Materials

Materials are based on fabric that measures 42" wide.

- 2 pieces, 8" x 9½", of mottled cream fabric for background and backing
- 1 strip, 2½" x 42", of light blue fabric for binding
- 1 strip, 2" x 22", of dark blue fabric for flowers
- 1 strip, 2" x 22", of light blue fabric for flowers
- 2 strips, 2" x 11", of green fabric for leaves
- 8" x 9½" piece of thin, dense batting
- Sewing thread to match fabrics
- 1 yard *each* of 2 different light green embellishing threads for large and small stems
- 15 white teardrop beads

As with "Bleeding Hearts" (page 70), I used just one thread for both stems: a multi-ply chenille. I used the entire thickness for the large stems and a single ply for the smaller stems that attach to the flowers.

Making the Quilt Top

UNLIKE A standard appliqué quilt, this project requires that you quilt and bind the quilt top before adding the appliquéd flowers. Work through the following steps, referring to "Basic Quilt Construction" (page 10) as needed.

1. Layer the backing, batting, and background squares.

2. Baste and quilt the layers, and then square the quilt to 6" x 7½".

3. Use the 2½" x 42" strip of light blue fabric to make the binding and finish the quilt edges.

Making the Flowers

1. Referring to "Making Hump-Shaped Petals" (page 16), layer the 2" x 22" strips of light blue and dark blue fabrics right sides together to make fifteen ¾" x ¾" petals. Cut out the petals, trimming close to the stitching at the top of the petal to reduce the bulk. Turn the petals right side out. Use caution when pushing out the tops of the petals; it's easy to push through the seam at the top. Finger-press the petals into shape with the seams centered in the front and back of the petal.

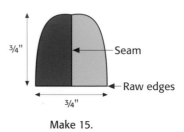

Make 15.

2. Finger-press a ⅛" hem around the bottom of each petal. Thread a hand-sewing needle with thread to match the dark blue fabric. Use a running stitch to gather the bottom of one petal; don't cut the thread. Instead, using the same thread, sew a running stitch all along the seam that joins the front and the back of the petal.

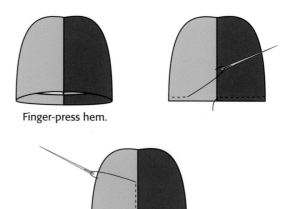

Finger-press hem.

3. Pull the sewing thread on the flower tightly to gather the flower into a heart shape. Stitch through the unit several times to lock the flower shape; knot the thread on the back of the flower. Sew a white teardrop bead to the bottom edge of the flower. Make 15 flowers.

Make 15.

Making the Leaves

REFERRING TO "Making Hump-Shaped Petals" (page 16), use the two 2" x 11" strips of green leaf fabric to make seven ¾" x ¾" hump-shaped leaves. Cut out the leaves and turn them right side out, finger-pressing them into shape. Turn up a ⅛" hem around the bottom of each leaf and finger-press. Use matching green thread to tightly gather the bottom of each leaf; knot the thread.

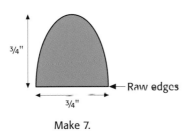

Make 7.

Finishing

REFER TO the quilt photo on page 73 as needed.

1. Referring to "Couching Threads for Embellishment" (page 23), couch the green embellishing threads to form the large and small stems.

2. Appliqué the seven leaves to the stems.

3. Appliqué the 15 flowers to the stems.

FOXGLOVES

I love the name of this flower: it makes me think of tiny foxes wearing elegant gloves as they run around in the woods. Foxgloves seem to defy the odds by growing in ditches along the busiest of freeways.

FINISHED SIZE: 6" x 9"

Materials

Materials are based on fabric that measures 42" wide.

- ◆ 2 pieces, 7" x 10", of mottled cream fabric for background and backing
- ◆ 1 strip, 2½" x 42", of pink batik fabric for binding
- ◆ 2 strips, 3" x 11", of pink batik fabric for flowers
- ◆ 2 strips, 2½" x 22", of pink batik fabric for flowers
- ◆ 1 strip, 2" x 15", of pink batik fabric for flowers
- ◆ 2 strips, 2½" x 11", of green fabric for leaves*
- ◆ 4 strips, 2½" x 22", of green fabric for calyxes*
- ◆ ¼ yard of green fabric for stems*
- ◆ 8" x 11" piece of thin, dense batting
- ◆ Bright pink fabric marking pen
- ◆ Dark pink fabric marking pen
- ◆ Water-soluble fabric glue
- ◆ Sewing thread to match fabric

These green fabrics may be the same.

Making the Quilt Top

UNLIKE A standard appliqué quilt, this project requires that you quilt and bind the quilt top before adding the appliquéd flowers. Work through the following steps, referring to "Basic Quilt Construction" (page 10) as needed.

1. Layer the backing, batting, and background squares.

2. Baste and quilt the layers, and then square the quilt to 6" x 9".

3. Use the 2½" x 42" strip of pink batik fabric to make the binding and finish the edges of the quilt.

Making the Flower Petals and Buds

1. Use the pattern on page 79 to make a large petal template. Referring to "Making Hump-Shaped Petals" (page 16), use the template to trace 10 large petals on the 3" x 11" strips of pink fabric. Sew and then cut out the petals, trimming close to the stitching at the top of the petal to reduce the bulk. Turn the petals right side out. Use caution when pushing out the tops of the petals; it's easy to push through the seam at the top. Finger-press the petals into shape.

2. Repeat step 1 using the medium petal pattern on page 79 and the 2½" x 22" strips of pink fabric to make 20 medium petals.

3. Use the bright pink fabric pen to mark elongated spots on the front of each petal. Allow the ink to dry. Use the dark pink fabric pen to add highlights and polka dots on each petal. Allow the ink to dry.

4. Cut the 2" x 15" strip of pink fabric into 10 1½" x 2" pieces.

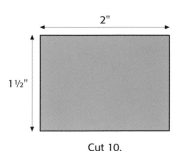

Cut 10.

5. Fold each piece of fabric in half with wrong sides together; finger-press. Fold the two upper corners inward as shown; finger-press.

Make 10.

6. Thread a hand-sewing needle with thread to match the pink fabric. Roll each folded unit from step 5 into a tube to make a bud as shown, tacking the bottom edge to secure. Pull the thread tightly to secure the shape; knot the thread. Make 10 flower buds.

Make 10.

Making the Leaves and Stems

1. Referring to "Making Basic Leaves" (page 19), use the two 2½" x 11" strips of green leaf fabric to make 15 leaves as shown. Each leaf shape should measure about ¾" wide at the bottom and 1¼" long. Cut out the leaves and turn them right side out, finger-pressing them into shape.

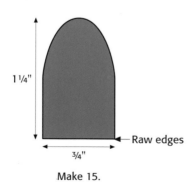

Make 15.

2. Referring to "Making Bias Tape" (page 18), use the green stem fabric to make 36" of ¼"-wide bias tape. Refer to the quilt photo on page 76 and cut the strips into five stems of varying lengths. Glue-baste the stems to the prepared background fabric, tucking the leaves from step 1 behind the stems. Make sure the raw edges of the leaves are covered by the stems.

3. Appliqué the stems in place, stitching through the leaves to attach them to the background.

Making the Calyxes

REFERRING TO "Making Hump-Shaped Petals" (page 16), use the four 2½" x 22" strips of green calyx fabric to make two strip sets. Use the strip sets to make 40 hump shapes to use as calyxes. Each calyx shape should measure about ¾" wide at the bottom and vary from ¾" to 1" long. Cut out the calyxes and turn them right side out. Finger-press a ⅛" hem around the bottom of each calyx.

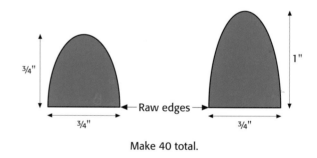

Make 40 total.

Assembling the Flowers
and Finishing the Quilt

REFER TO the quilt photo on page 76 as needed.

1. With the marked side facing up, fold the two sides of each large and medium flower petal toward the petal center, overlapping them slightly to make a flower as shown; baste. Insert each flower into a prepared calyx so the seams of the calyx are on the side of the flower, making sure all raw edges of the flower are covered. Using matching green thread, blindstitch the calyx to the flower, pulling the thread slightly to gather. Stitch through the unit several times to lock the shape; knot the thread on the back. Make 10 large and 20 medium flowers.

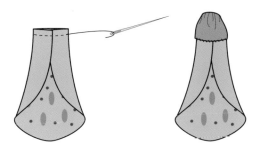

Make 10 large flowers
and 20 medium flowers.

2. Insert a flower bud into each remaining calyx. Using matching green thread, blindstitch the calyx to the bud, pulling the thread tightly to gather. Make 10 buds.

Make 10.

3. Blindstitch the 10 large flowers, 20 medium flowers, and 10 flower buds to the stems.

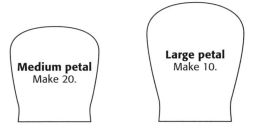

Medium petal
Make 20.

Large petal
Make 10.

STOCKS

Stocks are a great filler flower in a fabric bouquet. You'll need only small amounts of fabric to construct these easy flowers, so here is a good way to use those tiny scraps we quilters can't bear to throw away.

FINISHED SIZE: 6" x 9"

Materials

Materials are based on fabric that measures 42" wide.

- 2 pieces, 8" x 11", of mottled yellow fabric for background and backing
- 1 strip, 2" x 6", of purple fabric for large flowers
- 1 strip, 1½" x 21", of purple fabric for medium flowers
- 1 strip, 1" x 20", of purple fabric for small flowers
- 2 strips, 4" x 11", of green fabric for leaves
- ¼ yard of green fabric for stems
- 1 strip, 2½" x 42", of purple fabric for binding
- 8" x 11" piece of thin, dense batting
- Small piece of template material
- Sewing thread to match fabrics
- Water-soluble fabric glue
- 84 light purple seed beads
- ½ yard of light green embellishing thread for grass
- ½ yard of multicolored orange embellishing thread for grass

Making the Quilt Top

UNLIKE A standard appliqué quilt, this project requires that you quilt the quilt top before adding the appliquéd flowers. Work through the following steps, referring to "Basic Quilt Construction" (page 10) as needed.

1. Layer the backing, batting, and background squares.

2. Baste and quilt the layers, and then square the quilt to 6" x 9". Don't bind the quilt yet.

Making the Flowers

1. Use the pattern on page 82 to make a large stock flower template. Refer to "Making Yo-Yos" (page 22) and use the template to cut three circles, 2" in diameter, from the 2" x 6" strip of purple fabric. Make three tightly gathered large basic yo-yos for the large flowers.

2. Repeat step 1 using the medium stock flower pattern (page 82) and the 1½" x 21" strip of purple fabric to cut 14 circles, 1½" in diameter. Make 14 medium basic yo-yos for the medium flowers.

3. Repeat step 1 using the small stock flower pattern (page 82) and the 1" x 20" strip of purple fabric to cut 20 circles, 1" in diameter. Make 20 small basic yo-yos for the small flowers.

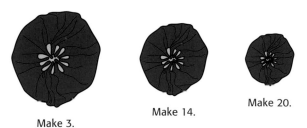

Make 3.   Make 14.   Make 20.

Making the Stems and Leaves

1. Referring to "Making Bias Tape" (page 18), use the green stem fabric to make 48" of ¼"-wide bias tape. Refer to the quilt photo on page 80 and cut the strips into seven stems of varying lengths. Glue-baste the stems to the prepared background fabric, aligning the raw edges of the stems with the raw edge of the quilt.

2. Referring to "Making Basic Leaves" (page 19), use the two 4" x 11" strips of green leaf fabric to make eight leaves as shown. Each leaf shape should measure about ¾" wide at the bottom and vary from 1" to 2" long. Cut out the leaves and turn them right side out, finger-pressing them into shape. Turn up a ⅛" hem around the bottom of each leaf and finger-press. Use matching green thread to tightly gather the bottom of each leaf; knot the thread. Make eight leaves.

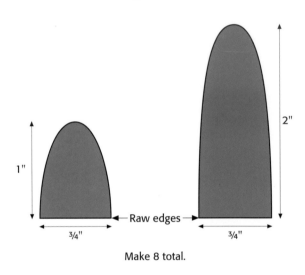

Make 8 total.

Finishing

REFER TO the quilt photo on page 80 as needed.

1. Appliqué the stems to the background fabric.

2. Referring to "Binding the Quilt" (page 12), use the 2½" x 42" strip of purple fabric to make the binding and finish the edges of the quilt. Make sure the raw edges of the stems are covered by the binding.

3. Stab stitch three light purple seed beads to the centers of the large and medium flowers and appliqué the flowers to the stems.

4. Stab stitch two beads to the centers of 13 small flowers and one bead to each remaining small flower. Appliqué the flowers with two beads to the stems and appliqué the flowers with one bead to the tops of the stems.

5. Appliqué the eight leaves to the stems.

6. Refer to "Couching Threads for Embellishment" (page 23). Twist the light green and multicolored orange embellishing threads together and couch the threads along the bottom of the stems to form the grass, leaving the ends of the embellishing threads to dangle for added texture.

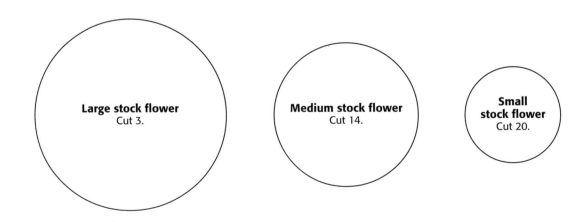

Large stock flower
Cut 3.

Medium stock flower
Cut 14.

Small stock flower
Cut 20.

LILACS

In early summer, the sweet smell of lilacs fills the air. Lilacs are an old-fashioned favorite in the garden. Make a bouquet for your sweetheart; these flowers look so real you can almost smell them.

FINISHED SIZE: 6½" x 11"

Materials

Materials are based on fabric that measures 42" wide.

- 2 pieces, 8½" x 13", of light green batik fabric for background and backing
- 1 strip, 2½" x 42", of light purple batik fabric for binding
- ¼ yard of green fabric for stems*
- 2 pieces, 4" x 6", of green fabric for large leaves*
- 2 strips, 3" x 18", of green fabric for medium leaves*
- 2 pieces, 2" x 8", of green fabric for small leaves*
- 2 strips, 2" x 42", of light purple batik fabric for large flowers
- 1 strip, 1½" x 42", of light purple batik fabric for medium flowers
- 1 strip, 1¼" x 15", of light purple batik fabric for small flowers
- 8½" x 13" piece of thin, dense batting
- Sewing thread to match fabrics
- ½ yard of sewable fusible web
- 225 light purple iridescent seed beads

These green fabrics may be the same.

Making the Quilt Top

UNLIKE A standard appliqué quilt, this project requires that you quilt and bind the quilt top before adding the appliquéd flowers. Work through the following steps, referring to "Basic Quilt Construction" (page 10) as needed.

1. Layer the backing, batting, and background squares.

2. Baste and quilt the layers, and then square the quilt to 6½" x 11".

3. Use the 2½" x 42" strip of light purple batik fabric to make the binding and finish the edges of the quilt.

Making the Stems and Leaves

1. Referring to "Making Bias Tape" (page 18), use the green stem fabric to make 36" of ¼"-wide bias tape. Refer to the quilt photo on page 83 and cut the strips into three stems of varying lengths. Appliqué the stems to the prepared background, making sure your stitches don't go through to the backing fabric.

2. Use the pattern on page 85 to make a template for the large leaf. Refer to "Making Fused Leaves" (page 20) and use the template, the 4" x 6" strips of green leaf fabric, and the fusible web to make two large leaves, following the diagram below for topstitching patterns. (Be sure to read the manufacturer's instructions for your particular fusible product.) Cut out the leaves. Refer to the quilt photo and tack-stitch the leaves to the stems.

3. Repeat step 2 using the medium leaf pattern (page 85) and the 3" x 18" strips of green leaf fabric to make six medium leaves. Topstitch, cut out, and tack-stitch each leaf to the stems.

4. Repeat step 2 using the small leaf pattern (page 85) and the 2" x 8" strips of green leaf fabric to make four small leaves. Topstitch, cut out, and tack-stitch each leaf to the stems.

Making and Appliquéing the Flowers

1. Use the pattern below to make a large lilac flower template. Refer to "Making Yo-Yos" (page 22) and use the template to cut 40 circles, 2" in diameter, from the 2" x 42" strips of light purple fabric. Make 40 tightly gathered basic yo-yos for the large flowers. Referring to the quilt photo, stab stitch three light purple seed beads in the center of each flower, and appliqué the flowers to the stems.

2. Repeat step 1 using the medium lilac flower pattern and the 1½" x 42" strip of light purple fabric to cut 25 circles, 1½" in diameter. Make 25 basic yo-yos for the medium flowers. Stab stitch three light purple seed beads in the center of each flower, and appliqué the flowers to the stems.

3. Repeat step 1 using the small lilac flower pattern and the 1¼" x 15" strip of light purple fabric to cut 10 circles, 1¼" in diameter. Make 10 basic yo-yos for the small flowers. Stab stitch three light purple seed beads in the center of each flower, and appliqué the flowers to the stems.

Large lilac leaf
Make 2.

Medium lilac leaf
Make 6.

Small lilac leaf
Make 4.

Large lilac flower
Cut 40.

Medium lilac flower
Cut 25.

Small lilac flower
Cut 10.

VIOLETS

The violet is much smaller than its close relative, the pansy.
The sweet scent of violets reminds me of my grandmother's perfume.

FINISHED SIZE: 6" x 5"

Materials

Materials are based on fabric that measures 42" wide.

- 2 pieces, 7" x 8", of tone-on-tone cream fabric for background and backing
- 1 strip, 2½" x 42", of purple batik fabric for binding
- 1 strip, 2½" x 22", of purple batik fabric for flowers and buds
- ¼ yard of green fabric for stems
- 2 strips, 2½" x 11", of green fabric for leaves and calyxes
- 7" x 8" piece of thin, dense batting
- Small piece of template material
- Sewing thread to match fabrics
- Purple fabric pen
- Yellow fabric pen
- 14 purple iridescent seed beads
- 7 yellow seed beads
- 1 yard of dark green embellishing thread for grass

Making the Quilt Top

UNLIKE A standard appliqué quilt, this project requires that you quilt and bind the quilt top before adding the appliquéd flowers. Work through the following steps, referring to "Basic Quilt Construction" (page 10) as needed.

1. Layer the backing, batting, and background squares.

2. Baste and quilt the layers, and then square the quilt to 6" x 5".

3. Use the 2½" x 42" strip of purple batik fabric to make the binding and finish the edges of the quilt.

Making the Flowers

1. Use the pattern on page 89 to make a violet flower template. Refer to "Making Yo-Yos" (page 22) and use the template to cut seven circles, 2½" in diameter, from the 2½" x 22" strip of purple fabric.

2. Use a circle to make a raw-edged yo-yo. Pull the thread to gather the circle tightly and take a few stitches to secure the gathers. Use your fingers to flatten and distribute the gathers; don't knot or cut the thread.

3. Push the needle through the center of the circle as shown (a). Pull the thread around one edge to the back of the circle, reinsert the needle into the center (b, c), and pull the thread tightly to gather the yo-yo. Repeat to gather the opposite edge (d).

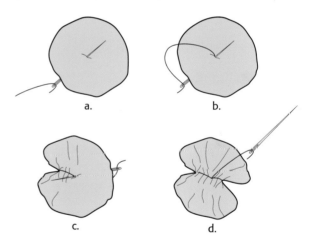

4. Pull the thread tightly over a third edge of the circle to form a three-lobed flower as shown. Stitch through the flower several times to lock in the flower shape; knot the thread.

5. Repeat steps 2 through 4 to make seven flowers.

6. Use the purple fabric pen to color the markings on the two upper lobes of the flowers as shown. Allow the ink to dry. Use the yellow fabric pen to color the marking on the bottom lobe of the flower. Allow the ink to dry.

7. Stab stitch two purple beads and one yellow bead to each flower.

Make 7.

Making the Stems and Leaves

1. Referring to "Making Bias Tape" (page 18), use the green stem fabric to make 36" of ¼"-wide bias tape. Fold the strips in half to measure ⅛" wide; press. Refer to the quilt photo on page 86 and cut the strips into seven stems of varying lengths. Appliqué the stems to the prepared background, making sure your stitches don't go through to the backing fabric.

2. Referring to "Making Basic Leaves" (page 19), use the two 2½" x 11" strips of green leaf fabric to make five leaves. Each leaf shape should measure about ½" wide at the bottom and 1¼" long. Cut out the leaves and turn them right side out, finger-pressing them into shape. Turn up a ⅛" hem around the bottom

of each leaf and finger-press. Use matching green thread to tightly gather the bottom of each leaf. Refer to the quilt photo and appliqué the bottom edge of each leaf to the flower stems.

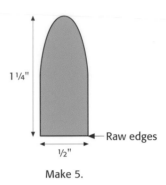

Make 5.

Making the Flower Buds and Calyxes

1. Cut the remaining purple flower fabric into two 1½" x 1½" squares. Fold each square in half with wrong sides together; finger-press. Fold the two upper corners to meet in the center as shown; finger-press.

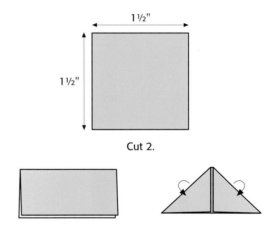

Cut 2.

2. Thread a hand-sewing needle with thread to match the purple fabric. Roll each folded unit from step 1 into a tube to make a bud as shown. Tack the raw edges, pulling the thread tightly to secure the shape; knot the thread. Make two buds.

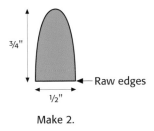

Make 2.

3. Referring to "Making Hump-Shaped Petals" (page 16), use the remaining leaf fabric to make two hump shapes to use as calyxes on the buds. Each calyx shape should measure about ½" wide and ¾" long. Cut out the calyxes and turn them right side out. Finger-press a ⅛" hem around the bottom of each calyx.

¾"

◄— Raw edges

½"

Make 2.

4. Insert each bud into a calyx, making sure the raw edges of the bud are covered. Use matching green thread to blindstitch the calyx to the bud, pulling the thread to gather slightly.

Make 2.

Finishing

REFER TO the quilt photo on page 86 as needed.

1. Appliqué the seven flowers to the tops of the stems.

2. Appliqué the two buds to the stems.

3. Referring to "Couching Threads for Embellishment" (page 23), couch the green embellishing thread to the bottom of the stems to form the grass, leaving the ends of the embellishing threads to dangle for added texture.

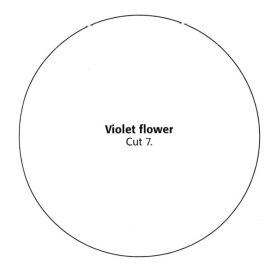

Violet flower
Cut 7.

COMMON PHLOX

This flower is so sweet, it reminds me of candy. A multicolored batik fabric really makes this flower beautiful.

FINISHED SIZE: 7" x 9½"

Materials

Materials are based on fabric that measures 42" wide.

- 2 pieces, 9" x 11½", of mottled yellow fabric for background and backing
- ¼ yard of green fabric for stems*
- 1 strip, 2½" x 42", of multicolored pink batik fabric for binding
- 1 strip, 2" x 42", of multicolored pink batik fabric for large flowers
- 1 strip, 1½" x 42", of multicolored pink batik fabric for medium flowers
- 1 strip, 1¼" x 42", of multicolored pink batik fabric for small flowers
- 2 strips, 2½" x 22", of green fabric for leaves*
- 9" x 11" piece of thin, dense batting
- Water-soluble fabric glue
- Small piece of template material
- Sewing thread to match fabrics
- 82 pink seed beads

These green fabrics may be the same.

Making the Quilt Top

UNLIKE A standard appliqué quilt, this project requires that you quilt the quilt top before adding the appliquéd flowers. Work through the following steps, referring to "Basic Quilt Construction" (page 10) as needed.

1. Layer the backing, batting, and background squares.

2. Baste and quilt the layers, and then square the quilt to 7" x 9½". Don't bind the quilt yet.

Making the Stems

1. Referring to "Making Bias Tape" (page 18), use the green stem fabric to make 36" of ¼"-wide bias tape. Refer to the quilt photo on page 90 and cut the strips into five stems of varying lengths. Glue-baste the stems to the prepared background fabric, aligning the raw edges of the stems with the raw edge of the quilt.

2. Appliqué the stems to the background fabric.

3. Referring to "Binding the Quilt" (page 12), use the 2½" x 42" strip of pink fabric to make the binding and finish the edges of the quilt. Make sure the raw edges of the stems are covered by the binding.

Making the Flowers

1. Use the pattern on page 92 to make a large phlox flower template. Refer to "Making Yo-Yos" (page 22) and use the template to cut 16 circles, 2" in diameter, from the 2" x 42" strips of pink fabric.

2. Use a circle to make a raw-edged yo-yo. Pull the thread to gather the circle tightly, and take a few stitches to secure the gathers. Use your fingers to flatten and distribute the gathers; don't knot or cut the thread.

3. Push the needle through the center of the circle as shown (a). Pull the thread around one edge to the back of the circle, reinsert the needle into the center (b, c), and pull the thread tightly to gather the yo-yo. Repeat to gather the opposite edge (d).

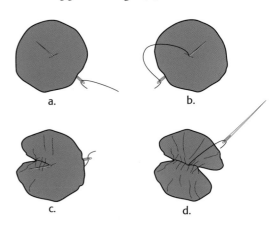

a.

b.

c.

d.

4. Repeat to gather the remaining two sides of the yo-yo, pulling the thread tightly to gather each lobe. Knot the thread on the back of the flower; don't cut the thread.

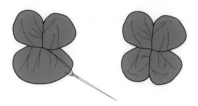

5. Stab-stitch a pink bead to the center of the flower; knot and cut the thread.

Make 16 large flowers.

6. Repeat steps 2 through 5 to make 16 large flowers.

7. Repeat steps 1 through 5 using the medium phlox flower pattern below and the 1½" x 42" strip of pink fabric to make 24 medium flowers.

8. Repeat steps 1 through 5 using the small phlox flower pattern below and the 1¼" x 42" strip of pink fabric to make 28 small flowers.

Making the Leaves

REFERRING TO "Making Basic Leaves" (page 19), use the two 2½" x 22" strips of green leaf fabric to make 14 leaves. Each leaf shape should measure about ¾" wide at the bottom and 1¼" long. Cut out the leaves and turn them right side out, finger-pressing them into shape. Turn up a ⅛" hem around the bottom of each leaf and finger-press. Use matching green thread to tightly gather the bottom of each leaf.

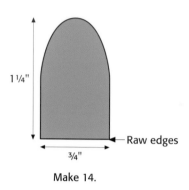

1¼"

Raw edges

¾"

Make 14.

Finishing

REFER TO the quilt photo on page 90 as needed.

1. Appliqué the flowers to the stems, starting with the large flowers at the bottom of the cluster and working up to the small flowers on the top.

2. Appliqué the bottom edge of the 14 leaves to the stems.

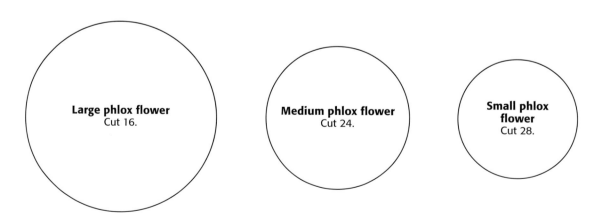

Large phlox flower
Cut 16.

Medium phlox flower
Cut 24.

Small phlox flower
Cut 28.

FALLING LEAVES

Fall is one of my favorite times of year. I look forward to the changing colors and the stormy weather. This project is a great way to use up leftover fabric.

FINISHED SIZE: 19" x 16"

Materials

Materials are based on fabric that measures 42" wide.

- 2 pieces, 18" x 21", of sky blue fabric for background and backing
- 2 strips, 2½" x 42", of dark blue fabric for binding
- 24 pieces, 4" x 12", of assorted fall-colored fabrics for leaves
- 18" x 21" piece of thin, dense batting
- 24 pieces, 4" x 6", of sewable fusible web
- Sewing thread to match fabrics

Making the Quilt Top

UNLIKE A standard appliqué quilt, this project requires that you quilt and bind the quilt top before adding the appliquéd leaves. Work through the following steps, referring to "Basic Quilt Construction" (page 10) as needed.

1. Layer the backing, batting, and background squares.

2. Baste and quilt the layers, and then square the quilt to 19" x 16".

3. Use the 2½" x 42" strips of dark blue fabric to make the binding and finish the edges of the quilt.

Making the Leaves and Finishing

REFER TO the quilt photo on page 93 as needed.

Use the leaf patterns on page 95 to make templates for three different leaf shapes. Refer to "Making Fused Leaves" (page 20) and use the templates, the 4" x 12" pieces of assorted fall-colored fabrics, and the 4" x 6" pieces of fusible web to make 24 leaves. Follow the patterns for guidance with topstitching. (Be sure to read the manufacturer's instructions for your particular fusible product.) Refer to the quilt photo and tack the leaves to the background, making sure your stitches don't go through to the backing fabric.

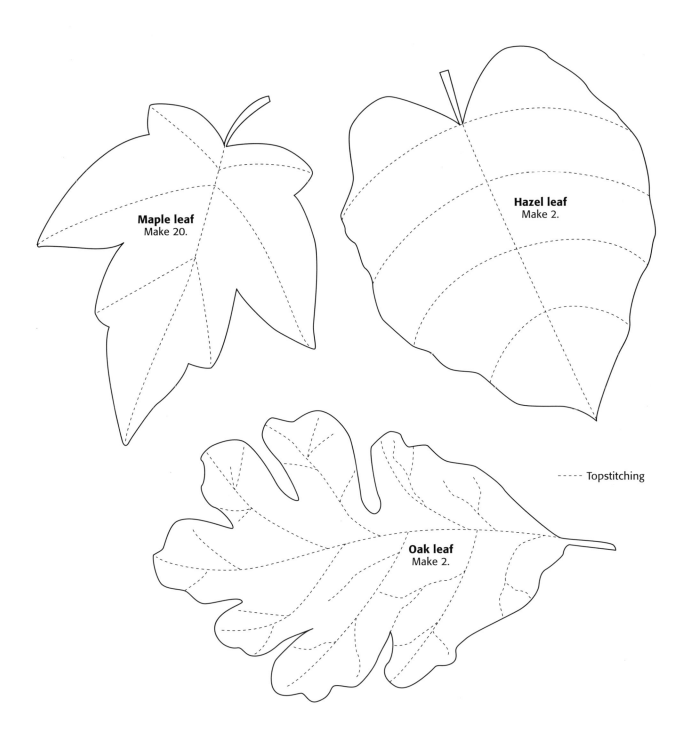

Maple leaf
Make 20.

Hazel leaf
Make 2.

---- Topstitching

Oak leaf
Make 2.

RESOURCES

For a wonderful selection of beads:

Shipwreck Beads
8560 Commerce Place Dr. NE
Lacey, WA 98516
1-800-950-4232
www.shipwreckbeads.com

For a wide range of embellishing threads and related notions:

Rainbow Gallery
7412 Fulton Ave., No. 5
North Hollywood, CA 91605
www.rainbowgallery.com
Rainbow Gallery doesn't offer mail order, but they'll direct you to stores in your area that carry their products.

ABOUT THE AUTHOR

SHARON BAKER'S love for gardening has enabled her to create realistic-looking flowers from fabric. She has spent hour after hour in the garden studying the complexities of nature. Having been born blind in her right eye, she sees the world in a very flat way. When working on an art project, she tries to incorporate some kind of three-dimensional element.

When Sharon discovered quilting, she knew she had finally found her artistic voice. She admits she is often obsessive and compulsive when she gets involved in any project. Making flowers out of fabric has become a driving passion.

Sharon is a relative newcomer to quilting, having started in 1999. Since then, quilting has consumed her life and she has worked at local quilt shops just to be closer to the fabric. She explains: "Thank goodness my husband and kids are used to my obsessive behavior. Otherwise I am sure my passion for fabric, beads, and embellishing threads would have made them crazy by now."

For workshop and lecture information, contact Sharon at: 18419 75th Ave. E
Puyallup, WA 98375-2341
ohsewcrazyone@yahoo.com